WHAT WOULD THE BIBLE SAY?

Biblical Answers to Everyday Challenges

Janice Hildreth

ADAMS MEDIA CORPORATION
AVON, MASSACHUSETTS

Published by
Adams Media Corporation
57 Littlefield Street, Avon, MA 02322. U.S.A.
www.adamsmedia.com

ISBN: 1-58062-924-5

Printed in Canada.

J I H G F E D C B A

Library of Congress Cataloging-in-Publication Data
Hildreth, Janice.
What would the Bible say? / Janice Hildreth.
p.   cm.
Includes bibliographical references.
ISBN 1-58062-924-5
1. Bible--Miscellanea. I. Title.
BS612.H55   2003
248.4--dc21   2003002715

This book is available at quantity discounts for bulk purchases.
For information, call 1-800-872-5627

*This book is lovingly dedicated to my husband, Michael,
who through twenty-nine years of marriage has always
encouraged my writing, comforted me in my disappointments
(even to hiding rejection slips on bad days), and believed in
my gift when I doubted it myself. All my love, always.*

PERMISSIONS

~

Unless otherwise annotated, all Scripture quotes are from the *New American Standard Bible*®. ©Copyright 1960, 1962, 1963, 1968, 1971, 1972, 1973, 1975, 1977, 1995 by The Lockman Foundation. Used by permission. (*www.Lockman.org*)

Scripture quotations marked "AMP" are taken from the *Amplified Bible*. Copyright ©1954, 1958, 1962, 1964, 1965, 1987 by The Lockman Foundation. Used by permission.

Scripture quotations marked "NIV" are taken from the *Holy Bible International Version*® NIV R. Copyright ©1973, 1978, 1984 by International Bible Society. Used by permission of Zondervan. All rights reserved.

Scripture quotations marked "NKJV" are taken from the *New King James Version*. Copyright ©1982 by Thomas Nelson, Inc. Used by permission. All rights reserved.

Scripture quotations marked "NLT" are taken from the *Holy Bible, New Living Translation*. Copyright ©1996. Used by permission of Tyndale House Publishers, Inc., Wheaton, IL 60189, USA. All rights reserved.

Scripture quotations marked "CEV" are taken from the *Contemporary English Version*. Copyright ©1995 American Bible Society.

Scripture quotations marked "KJV" are taken from the *King James Version*. Copyright ©1989 World Bible Pub. Co.

CONTENTS

~

ACKNOWLEDGMENTS

~

I would like to give a special thank-you to my whole family who, all but dancing in the streets, celebrated with me the joy of signing my first book contract. To my immediate family, Michael, Jana, David, and Jennifer, I want to say thanks for your forbearance in living with "the book" for four months. (Yes, Jenny, *now* we can talk.) Thanks, Mom, for always believing I would do it. Thanks, too, for your proofreading skills—that schoolteacher's eye never rests. Much love to my mentor and big sister, Mary Ann Wilkie, for her encouragement and the example of her life. A special thank-you goes to the weekly lunch ladies. You met faithfully with me to talk out the philosophy and advice of this book, editing and encouraging 'til the eleventh hour (literally). I also wish to say thank you to former Adams Media Executive Editor, Claire Gerus, who saw potential in my writing and pushed open a door for me; and for my editors, Tracy Quinn McLennan and Kate Epstein, who gently edited my prose into readable form. "I thank my God always, making mention of you in my prayers" (Philemon 1:4).

God bless,
Janice Hildreth
Fall 2003

INTRODUCTION

~

I believe the best resource for practical living is the Bible.
The Holy Scriptures offer the sanest, most practical guidelines for our lives. Within its covers are clear, satisfying solutions for every quandary. I often hear popular opinions
accepted as truth by the young people I encounter. When I
point out that the Bible often doesn't support popular opinion or accepted standards of behavior, they are surprised.
They assume that because the Scriptures do not use modern
terms such as euthanasia or abortion, that it therefore is silent
on many of the issues people are facing in the twenty-first
century.

However, the Bible, inspired by God, given as a guide-
book to His people, has the ability to relate to any culture
and situation. This is because our omnipotent God, knowing
that vocabulary and modes of behavior would alter with the
passing of time, created infallible principles within Scripture.
Biblical principles are fundamental truths that transcend culture and historical eras and are applicable for any society and
generation. When we understand the Bible's principles, we
have the key to gaining God's perspective on any situation.

As a pastor's wife for twenty-four years, it has been my
heart's desire to teach people about the Bible's relevancy. I
have seen firsthand the chaos that results from people who
live their lives by relying on feelings and popular opinion for
direction. I long for everyone to understand that who God is
and what He desires is encapsulated in the principles that
govern His nature, and that these truths can be applied to

any situation we are facing. In this book, I have compiled commonly-asked questions about life from contemporary Christians. I have drawn upon the experience acquired through two decades of working in the marketplace, pastoring churches with my husband, and meeting people online on my Web site. The questions are those verbalized at the workplace, in magazine articles, over backyard fences, on news programs, and from day-to-day interaction with peers. They reflect the inner struggle many Christians face when they attempt to live out their Christianity with integrity and truth. To further illustrate the biblical soundness of each answer, I include an Old Testament and New Testament Scripture that validates each answer. While inevitably my opinion is reflected, the Scriptures demonstrate the biblical soundness of my response.

Jesus said, "Yesterday, today and forever I am the same." The advice is already written. I simply applied it within the context of modern living.

Janice Hildreth
2003

SPIRITUALITY

1. I am told by unbelievers that too many years have passed since the Bible was written for it to be a reliable source. They point out that since original Scriptures had to be copied by hand, inaccuracies had to have occurred. How can I defend the Bible's integrity?

I understand their skepticism, but my first reaction is to say, if that is true, why do the Scriptures still work? Today we can still read the Bible and feel the assurance of the Holy Spirit in our heart. We can practice the principles and have them bless our lives. We can believe the promises and see miracles occur. When we pray, people are healed. When we ask God for the answer to a problem for which there appears to be none, He brings one about. So I ask again, if it is not valid, why has it validated so many lives?

Beyond that, the authenticity of the Scriptures has documentation: the Dead Sea Scrolls, found in the mid-1900s, are one example. When the written Scripture was first copied, the churchmen who copied it realized it was a legacy and a commandment from God Himself and took their job extremely seriously. They spent years meticulously creating exact duplications.

∾ *Every word of God is tested; He is a shield to those who take refuge in Him. (Proverbs 30:5)*
∾ *All Scripture is inspired by God and profitable for teaching, for reproof, for correction, for training in righteousness. (2 Timothy 3:16)*

~

2. If we are children of God, why do we need His protection?

*W*e need God's hand of protection because the Bible warns us that the enemy of our souls roams about seeking to destroy us. God has given this world to Satan's dominion for a time; Christians need to ask for God's protection every day. Some people believe that since they are Christians, nothing bad can happen to them. That is erroneous thinking. God certainly does protect us and often we are not aware of it. Safeguarding us is a primary responsibility of the angels. However, trusting God does not mean we have a lucky rabbit's foot, or that we will always lead a charmed life. Terrible things do sometimes happen to God's people. It is a result of living in a sinful world. We need to keep our eyes on God and trust that even when hard times come, or should bad things happen, He will be right there to go through it with us.

∾ *For He will give His angels charge concerning you, to guard you in all your ways. (Psalms 91:11)*
∾ *Your adversary, the devil, prowls around like a roaring lion, seeking someone to devour. (1 Peter 5:8)*

∼

3. As long as I believe in God, joining a church really isn't important, is it?

The importance of a church lies in the fact that it offers spiritual nourishment for each member of your family. While Christianity is an individual experience, it is lived out as part of a body. The Bible commands us not to be spiritual Lone Rangers, for we are vulnerable when separated from our brothers and sisters. In the same manner that a body without one of its limbs is limited in its effectiveness, we become unbalanced by not joining ourselves to a local church body.

Joining a church will not get you into Heaven, but it does provide vital resources for your spiritual growth. A church provides guidance, teaching, training, and fellowship. It is a community that will love, support, and encourage you. The members will be there during your children's toddler years when you wonder if you will survive, provide encouragement and humor when you and your teens face adolescence, and comfort you when tragedies occur. In our transient society, a church is the one common link that provides continuity from community to community. You may not know your next-door neighbors, but you do know you will meet "family" when you step inside the front door of your new church your first Sunday in town.

∾ *I was glad when they said to me, "Let us go to the house of the LORD." (Psalms 122:1)*
∾ *Not forsaking the assembling of ourselves together, as the manner of some is; but exhorting one another: and so much the more, as ye see the day approaching. (Hebrews 10:25 KJV)*

4. As long as I live an honest moral life, that is all that God requires of me, right?

*C*hrist knew that no matter how hard we would try to be good, we would need a savior. That is why He came to die for our sins. In the Book of Revelation there is a story about a church in the town of Laodocia. That church was like many good people today. They looked at themselves and said, "We have got it made. We are wealthy, and there isn't anything we need." But God looked at them and said, "You are not rich. You actually are wretched, miserable, poor, blind, and naked."

While your life may appear adequate to you, you are using the wrong gauge for measuring. God's Word is the standard. Without God we are all sinners. We all need a savior.

How much better to be a double winner by accepting that you need salvation through Jesus Christ, and *then* live your life according to His principles. By doing this, you will still be a positive influence on society and also gain Eternal Life.

～ *For all of us have become like one who is unclean, and all our righteous deeds are like a filthy garment; and all of us wither like a leaf, and our iniquities, like the wind, take us away. (Isaiah 64:6)*
～ *For all have sinned and fall short of the glory of God. (Romans 3:23)*

～

5. Is there a difference between wisdom and knowledge?

*Y*es, knowledge is the accumulation of facts, but wisdom is the ability to correctly discern and use the facts. Wisdom comes as a divine gift from God. Often we know people who are very intelligent and knowledgeable and yet do not seem to know how to pass along this information. They make very poor teachers and are often irritating in their arrogance. Wisdom, on the other hand, intuitively understands how to meld information and to impart it. Knowledge deals only with facts, but wisdom follows the Holy Spirit's leading by acting on unseen, even unknown, information to make choices. Wisdom sometimes seems at odds with knowledge, but that is because God knows what lies ahead and understands the correct path we should take.

～ *Only the LORD give thee wisdom and understanding. (1 Chronicles 22:12 KJV)*
～ *But if any of you lacks wisdom, let him ask of God, who gives to all generously and without reproach, and it will be given to him. (James 1:5)*

6. I do not feel God when I pray. What am I doing wrong?

I am sure you are not doing anything wrong; you may just need some guidance and reassurance. First of all, you need to know that God longs to communicate with you. His greatest desire is to have an intimate relationship with you. Nothing gives Him greater joy than to hear you call on Him.

However, it takes practice to know that you are hearing God's voice. The longer you work on your relationship with Him, the better skilled you will become at "hearing" His voice. One reason you may not feel God when you pray is that you do not know what to look for. So let's start from the beginning:

• Each time you pray, examine your life and ask God to reveal any unrepentant sin. Sin creates a barrier between us and God that will hinder communication. If something is revealed, immediately ask Him to forgive you for it.

• Next, begin to speak to Him as if He were sitting right next to you. If this is very new, sit in a chair and place an empty chair next to you, then turn toward it as if Jesus were sitting there, and begin speaking to Him. When you do this you are displaying faith. "What is faith? It is the confident assurance that something we desire is going to happen. It is the certainty that what we hope for is waiting for us even though we cannot see it up ahead" (Hebrews 11:1 NLT). This Scripture tells us that if we want to know that God hears us, we need to believe that He is listening. So, go ahead and talk; tell Him everything. He wants to know it all.

• Then, like all good conversations, take time to listen to Him. Sit quietly after you speak and allow a few minutes of silence in which He can respond to you. It will come as a thought in your mind and follow with a sense of His presence.

• Finally, do not place too much emphasis on feelings. Because we are human, feelings come and go depending on our circumstances, our health, and whatever else is going on in our lives. God does not play games with us. Even on days He feels far away, He is not. He never leaves us.

❧ *Praise be to the LORD, for he has heard my cry for mercy. (Psalms 28:6 NIV)*
❧ *And without faith it is impossible to please Him, for he who comes to God must believe that He is and that He is a rewarder of those who seek Him. (Hebrews 11:6)*

~

7. Every day I ask my husband if we can have devotions together, but he always has an excuse. How can I get him to pray with me?

From my experience, I believe that the majority of Christian husbands do not pray with their wives. I want to be quick and point out that I am *not* saying they do not pray. Instead, it probably shows that men may be aware of how much better some women are at communicating verbally, and they may feel inadequate in their stumbling sentences. I encourage you not to make your desire a point of contention. Instead, simply assure him every day that you are praying for him and faithfully carry it out. Individual spiritual growth is the job of the Holy Spirit in each of our lives. When your husband does pray with you, be sure to thank him sincerely and let him know how much it means to you to hear him pray out loud. Be full of hope for the day when he will join you in prayer.

❧ *She brings him good, not harm, all the days of her life. (Proverbs 31:12 NIV)*
❧ *A wife should put her husband first, as she does the Lord. (Ephesians 5:22 CEV)*

8. We are thinking of joining a church. What should we look for in choosing a church?

A church provides vital support to your Christian life. You need to choose one carefully and then commit to it, because a church is like your family. When you have disagreements, please do not leave. If you will stay and work them out, it will bring maturing for both you and other members.

The first criterion will be to find one whose teachings correlate with your beliefs or you will counteract the reason for going to church in the first place. Most churches have doctrinal statements available to visitors, or they will be glad to mail you one, which list their foundational beliefs.

The next two considerations are practical: What programs does it offer and how close is it to your home? You should choose a church in your area. If you have to travel over an hour to get to it, you may be hesitant to participate in the programs and activities—which will negate why you joined in the first place. However, when you look at the programs, do not place too much emphasis on them, as programs come and go. Besides, maybe the very program you are looking for is one that God would like you to start in this church yourself. Remember, in a family everybody shares the work.

Above all, pray about your decision and follow the leading of the Holy Spirit. I usually encourage people to join a small or medium-size church. In smaller churches we more easily realize the importance each of us has in the body of Christ and the part we bring to its function. Sometimes in a large church there is a temptation to become a bench warmer because it appears your help is not necessary. Christianity is not a spectator sport, so be a participatant.

∾ *I was glad when they said to me, "Let us go to the house of the LORD." (Psalms 122:1)*
∾ *But now God has placed the members, each one of them, in the body, just as He desired. (1 Corinthians 12:18)*

9. What does it mean when God does not answer my prayers?

Prayers do not go unanswered; it only seems that way to our finite minds. God has promised to hear us when we call on Him. In Revelation it describes a scene in Heaven in which there are golden bowls full of incense that are the prayers of the saints. So not only does He always hear us, He actually saves up our prayers. We must be born again before we qualify as "saints" and we must ask according to His will. It is not wrong to ask for something for ourselves, but what is the condition of our heart in general? Are we walking with the Lord daily and living according to His word? He is not simply the candy man in the sky who rules and reigns simply to satisfy our insatiable need for things and self-gratification. He loves us, but sometimes the answer is "no." Certainly for those of us who are earthly parents, we understand that all of the requests made by our children are not in their best interest and therefore we also say "no." Other times it may be a matter of timing. At times we say, "When you are older." I think that sometimes God wants us to grow up in Him. Just as we use life lessons to teach our children because we love them, so too does God. It does not matter how much a child wants something, we will not give permission for it if we feel it isn't in the child's best interest. We must allow God to be God. One of the most important things about prayer is that we must trust Him. How can we trust Him with eternity if we cannot trust Him today?

I encourage everyone with whom I talk to keep a prayer journal. Write down your prayer requests and each month go back and see how many of them God has taken care of. It may take years for you to see the result of some of your prayers, but do not despair; God has your prayers in a bowl in the throne room.

~ *God is our refuge and strength, a very present help in trouble. (Psalms 46:1–2)*

∾ *You ask and do not receive, because you ask with wrong motives, so that you may spend it on your pleasures. (James 4:3)*

~

10. I feel like such a failure as a Christian. I do not do anything I promise myself I will do. Then, everything I swear I'll never do again entraps me before I know it. What am I doing wrong?

I fully understand your dilemma because I, too, struggle with it. Actually, the Apostle Paul spoke about it. I would say it is a condition common to all of us. Within us are two warring natures: our old sinful nature (the habits and natural tendencies we have) and our Christian life. Each day we are given the opportunity to glorify God in our life or to take the path of least resistance and do what comes naturally. That is why is it so important that we begin each day by putting on God's armor. You will find it listed in Ephesians, chapter 6. God says if we don the armor of truth, righteousness, peace, faith, salvation, and God's Word, we will be able to defend ourselves against Satan's schemes.

As we daily deny our old nature and lean on God, we will find habits that have ensnared us for years begin to loosen their grip. The important thing to remember is to keep seeking God and keep trying.

∾ *He keeps the feet of His godly ones, but the wicked ones are silenced in darkness; for not by might shall a man prevail. (1 Samuel 2:9)*
∾ *For I do not understand my own actions [I am baffled, bewildered]. I do not practice or accomplish what I wish, but I do the very thing that I loathe [which my moral instinct condemns]. (Romans 7:15 AMP)*

11. Is drinking alcohol sinful?

The practice of drinking alcohol is not condemned in the Bible. Contrary to what many have believed, it is very doubtful that people in biblical times drank grape juice, for the simple reason that there was no refrigeration to keep it from fermenting. What the Bible does condemn is drunkenness. If you drink in moderation, there is nothing wrong with your practice. However, keep in mind Christ's admonition not to harm someone's weaker conscience. We are our brother's keeper, and, therefore, we are not to indulge in practices that others consider wrong when they are around us.

For myself, when I considered those individuals' backlash of tragedy that follows in the wake of social drinking, I had to say it was not worth the chance of becoming addicted to it. The old rube that states "if you never drink you'll never become an alcoholic" is certainly true. Many AA members wish they had never started. Addictions are terrifying and relentless. If you can stop the chance of it happening to you, or those you love by your example, why not?

꙾ *Wine is a mocker, strong drink a brawler, and whoever is intoxicated by it is not wise. (Proverbs 20:1)*
꙾ *All things are lawful, but not all things are profitable. All things are lawful, but not all things edify. (1 Corinthians 10:23)*

12. Do we really have a guardian angel?

Angels are real beings who do God's bidding. Their primary function is to be an army that fights evil. They have real bodies that are similar to human form. However, the Scriptures do not seem to indicate that any are assigned permanently to one person to protect, except maybe in the case of children. Matthew 18:10 says, "See that you do not look down on one of these little ones. For I tell you that their angels in Heaven always see the face of my Father in Heaven." However, if only children are assigned a personal angel, we still do not need to fear that we are left vulnerable. Angels are sent wherever the need for protection of God's people arises. In truth, angels are not the gentle creatures pictured today but fearsome warriors.

∾ *For He will give His angels charge concerning you, to guard you in all your ways. (Psalms 91:11)*
∾ *Be not forgetful to entertain strangers: for thereby some have entertained angels unawares. (Hebrews 13:2 KJV)*

∾

13. My friend's mom died. She went to see a medium who told her she could communicate with her mom. I am sure that is not wise; what can I say to her?

Your friend is understandably seeking emotional healing. There is a great gulf between our life and eternity. Unfortunately, demons can take on many guises and even imitate people. That is why the Scripture clearly instructs us not to have anything to do with fortunetellers. They can lead us into false security and demonic activity. As the Prophet Isaiah said, "Why would you consult the dead for advice for the living?" (Isaiah 8:19).

In order to help her, lend a listening ear and ask God for wisdom to perceive what is driving her to communicate with her mother. No doubt she misses her and wants to speak to her again, but that may not be the whole reason. Maybe she is carrying guilt for the "what ifs" everyone has for missed opportunity. She needs to know about God's grace and peace, which can heal that hurt. It could be that she is frightened about the hereafter and she wants to know what's out there. She may think that if she could communicate with her mother, she could gain some knowledge about life after death. So you could share with her the hope that is found in Jesus Christ and the Eternal Life that He offers believers.

So do not listen to your prophets, your diviners, your interpreters of dreams, your mediums or your sorcerers . . . (Jeremiah 27:9 NIV)

But for the cowardly and unbelieving and abominable and murderers and immoral persons and sorcerers and idolaters and all liars, their part will be in the lake that burns with fire and brimstone, which is the second death. (Revelation 21:8)

~

14. I've heard people talk about fasting when they have wanted an answer from God. Does that work?

Yes. There is something about denying our physical appetites that makes our spiritual ears more perceptive to God's voice. Fasting helps us gain insight into God's plan. When we fast, we more clearly perceive His will. Sometimes we fast to bring about a result promised by God but whose fulfillment seems to be hindered. Fasting can bring down the barrier that is keeping the answer from coming. At other times we may fast to increase our intimacy with God.

Fasting involves more than just refraining from eating. When we fast we need to concentrate on praying and reading our Bible, for fasting and prayer go together. When you choose to fast, have a specific purpose in mind and set a specific time limit for your fast. Many spiritual battles are won by fasting. One other practical admonition about fasting is that we are not to call attention to ourselves when we fast.

∞ *Is not this the fast that I have chosen? To loose the bands of wickedness, to undo the heavy burdens, and to let the oppressed go free, and that ye break every yoke? (Isaiah 58:6 KJV)*

∞ *Whenever you fast, do not put on a gloomy face as the hypocrites do, for they neglect their appearance so that they will be noticed by men when they are fasting. Truly I say to you, they have their reward in full. But you, when you fast, anoint your head and wash your face so that your fasting will not be noticed by men, but by your Father who is in secret; and your Father who sees what is done in secret will reward you. (Matthew 6:16–18)*

~

15. Are demons real? If so, were they really angels once?

Yes, demons are real beings that dwell with Satan and try to turn everyone away from God. They live in an evil spirit world and their sole purpose is to thwart God's plan and deceive people. Jude, verse 6, tells us that they were once angels in Heaven but joined Satan in his rebellion against God and as a consequence were cast out of Heaven with him.

In resisting Satan and his demons, do not give them or him any more credit than is their due. For example, they are not omnipresent; they can only be in one place at one time. They are not omniscient; they cannot read your mind. Neither are they omnipotent; they do not have unlimited power.

However, that does not mean they are powerless. While God has given them dominion over the earth, they are allowed only limited access to your life—access that either you or God gives them. Do not dwell on them but rather keep your eyes on Jesus, the author and finisher of our faith.

He will give you the strength to face any attack by the enemy of our souls.

∾ *The LORD said to Satan, "Have you considered My servant Job? For there is no one like him on the earth, a blameless and upright man, fearing God and turning away from evil." (Job 1:8)*
∾ *The demons began to entreat Him, saying, "If You are going to cast us out, send us into the herd of swine." (Matthew 8:31)*

~

16. I always read my horoscope because I consider it a joke. A Christian friend recently saw me reading it and was unbelievably horrified. Isn't she over-reacting?

Sometimes Scripture is vague on matters of conscience, but in the case of supernatural phenomenon, Leviticus (19:26 AMP) states that horoscopes are something we are strictly forbidden to use. We dwell in a universe of two spirit worlds: good and evil. Any supernatural power comes from one of two sources: God or Satan. The Bible tells us that God is a jealous God, meaning that He refuses to share what is rightfully His with anyone or anything. Horoscopes fall under the power of demonic activity.

I understand that you believe as long as you do not take them seriously, they are just a harmless activity. However, by reading horoscopes you open a window of opportunity for satanic activity. Whatever we put into our minds becomes a permanent part of our being. As an example, let's say that today your horoscope reads: "Beware of financial transactions." If you later mislay a $20 bill, what will no doubt come into your mind? Would it be the message from your horoscope? Satan is very good at manipulating circumstances for his purposes. Once something is planted in your mind, he can use it to begin to play mind games with you.

∾ *You shall not eat anything with the blood; neither shall you use magic, omens, or witchcraft [or predict events by horoscope or signs and lucky days]. (Leviticus 19:26 AMP)*

∾ *As we were on our way to the place of prayer, we were met by a slave girl who was possessed by a spirit of divination [claiming to foretell future events and to discover hidden knowledge], and she brought her owners much gain by her fortunetelling. . . . And she did this for many days. Then Paul, being sorely annoyed and worn out, turned and said to the spirit within her, I charge you in the name of Jesus Christ to come out of her! And it came out that very moment. (Acts 16:16, 18 AMP)*

~

17. I have always tried to be a good person but still worry about being good enough to go to Heaven. Therefore, it surely is not true that all a drug dealer, child molester, or serial killer has to do to go to Heaven is ask for forgiveness. Isn't God a God of justice?

Yes, God is a just God. This means He exacts the same requirements from everyone for citizenship in Heaven. To be able to pass through Heaven's gates requires only one thing: salvation. Our passport is issued when we accept Jesus Christ as our Savior. All the good things we do in our life have nothing to do with salvation. And conversely, no amount of "bad" things can exclude us if we are willing to confess our sins and ask for forgiveness.

This being the case, you will not meet any drug dealers, child molesters, or serial killers in Heaven. The Bible tells us that when we are born again we become new creations.

Since all the old sin falls away, whom you may meet in Heaven will only be a *former* drug dealer, child molester, or a serial killer. No matter what they were before salvation, they are not that now. We are all sinners saved by grace.

∾ *Our righteousnesses are as filthy rags. (Isaiah 64:6 KJV)*
∾ *Can we boast then, that we have done anything to be accepted by God? No, because our acquittal is not based on our good deeds. It is based on our faith. (Romans 3:27 NLT)*

18. I have a friend who often relates media and e-mail stories she has heard. When I do not see them substantiated by other sources, I question their validity. I am convinced that we should have proof before we believe rumors.

Stories such as you describe are called urban legends. No one knows who starts them, but they seem to self-generate. You are right to question them, for if you should pass them on only to have to discount them later, your naiveté will weaken your message on other issues. They have proliferated since the 1960s when Madalyn Murray O'Hair was supposedly trying to take Christian programming off the air. Later reports said that Oprah (Donohue, Leno—you pick one) was giving 10 percent of her earnings to the Satanist church. More recent ones center around fear and hype arising from the bombing of the World Trade Centers.

The Bible says we are to be as wise as serpents and as harmless as doves. Undocumented stories are not harmless. They feed on fears and make us emotional victims. Naiveté is not considered a good characteristic in the Bible. God instructs us to act wisely. There are plenty of documented cases without passing along undocumented ones. If you receive e-mails or are told a story that seems outlandish, check it out before you pass it on. For more information on seeking truth in our society's stories, see the CitizenLink Web site listed in the bibliography.

The bottom line is that since we serve the God of Truth, speaking truth needs to be extremely important to us.

∾ *The naive believes everything, but the sensible man considers his steps. (Proverbs 14:15)*
∾ *Professing to be wise, they became fools. (Romans 1:22)*

~

19. My baby died when she was six months old as a result of crib death. Why would God do that to me? My husband and I are devastated, our marriage is on the rocks, and I am angry. Will I ever feel normal again?

I cannot begin to imagine the pain that you are experiencing. I am sure you already intuitively know that you will never feel "normal" again, in that you cannot return to the life you lived before you had your child. I understand that the death of a child brings pain that must be inconsolable. However, I do know someone who would like very much to comfort you. Your child died because of sin's dominion in the world, of which death is a very real part. However, while she lived, she lived the full span of time that God decreed for her. Because it was only a length of six months does not make it any less of a viable and significant life.

I'd like to reassure you regarding the tension in your marriage. What you and your husband are experiencing is a normal reaction of grief. Please do not allow your relationship to disintegrate because you each feel the other is not acting correctly. Give yourselves time to grieve and understand that grief is personal and processed differently by each person. You cannot circumvent the grieving process. There are specific stages of grief, and, unfortunately, they have to be experienced in order to heal. (See Chapter 3, Question 19, for the specific stages.)

More than anything, besides just throwing yourself into the arms of God and weeping, the best help you can give yourself will be to join a support group. If your husband does not wish to join, go for yourself. It will give insight, direction, and comfort. (Also, see the bibliography for resources on death.)

∽ *He heals the brokenhearted and binds up their wounds. (Psalms 147:3)*
∽ *For the Lord Himself will descend from Heaven with a shout, with the voice of the archangel and with the trumpet of God, and the dead in Christ will rise first. Then we who are alive and remain will be caught up together with them in the clouds to meet the Lord in the air, and so we shall always be with the Lord. Therefore comfort one another with these words. (1 Thessalonians 4:16–18)*

∽

20. You seem to indicate that all good attributes come from God, which would lead me to expect His followers would be the most wonderful people I will meet. Yet, I personally know many unbelievers whose lives reflect better character traits than those of Christians. How can you explain it?

I will continually stress in this book the importance of applying biblical principles to your life. Attributes such as honesty, kindness, and compassion are attributes of God that may come as a spiritual awakening, but they can also be deliberately implemented through self-discipline. When someone exhibits any one of these attributes, their inherent benefits will bless that person whether or not they are followers of God.

They are, in effect, self-fulfilling prophecies. For example, no matter what your motive is for being kind, when you show kindness to others, you will reap kindness back on yourself, as demonstrated by the principle of sowing and reaping.

It is a self-evident fact that goodness benefits society and makes life more comfortable. The only drawback is that demonstrating godly character by our own willpower does not give us any eternal value. How much wiser we are to allow the Holy Spirit to produce the eternal fruit of love, joy, peace, longsuffering, gentleness, goodness, meekness, temperance, faith. This will give you benefits in this life and after life.

~ *Those who plant seeds of injustice will harvest disaster, and their reign of terror will end. (Proverbs 22:8 NLT)*
~ *For by grace you have been saved through faith; and that not of yourselves, it is the gift of God. (Ephesians 2:8)*

~

21. I have made some very bad choices in my life, some of which still cause me pain whenever I think of them. My problem is that I think of them a lot. I cannot get them out of my mind, and I have a hard time believing that God has really forgiven me. How can I get past my guilt and know I am forgiven?

You are right when you say it is hard to feel forgiven when we contemplate some of the sins we have committed. However, just because we do not feel that something is true does not make it untrue. Emotions are notoriously unreliable, particularly in the area of feeling forgiven.

Whenever I come into conflict with the way God says something is and the way I feel about it, I have made it a practice to memorize Scripture instead. The Bible is an actual spiritual weapon. It can be used to fight Satan.

Get a concordance and look up a word or words that describes the issue you are struggling with. After each entry is a list of Scriptures that speak to that issue. Take your Bible and look up each verse until you find one that seems to speak to your situation and spirit. Memorize it. Whenever Satan comes whispering accusations against you, speak that verse back to him. Do not allow your mind to dwell on the accusations. Instead, focus on the promise in that Scripture. At first it may seem like an empty activity, but I guarantee that Satan cannot stay when you use God's Word as a weapon against him. One day you'll say, "Wow! I do not struggle with that anymore; that is cool!"

Finally, you need to forgive yourself. Leave your past behind and face the future knowing you are forgiven and set free from sin.

∽ *As far as the east is from the west, so far has He removed our transgressions from us. (Psalms 103:12)*
∽ *Therefore there is now no condemnation for those who are in Christ Jesus. (Romans 8:1)*

~

22. I didn't have a father in my life. How can I view God as my Father when I never knew what one was like?

*T*hink about what the example of a perfect father would be. One who is loving, caring, and always ready to listen. He would be compassionate and gentle toward His children. You could trust His strength knowing He would always protect you and provide for your needs. Then remember how God established all truths. He did it just like any good parent does; He made himself the example.

It might be easier to first think of God as your closest friend, the one you call on day or night, the one you know will be there no matter the circumstances. Use Christ, who may appear more approachable in Scripture, as the example of God's attributes. Then, as you establish that relationship, allow the Holy Spirit to do the work of turning it into a beautiful father-child bond.

∽ *A father of the fatherless . . . Is God in His holy habitation. (Psalms 68:5)*
∽ *Jesus said to him, "Have I been so long with you, and yet you have not come to know Me, Philip? He who has seen Me has seen the Father; how can you say, 'Show us the Father'? "Do you not believe that I am in the Father, and the Father is in Me? The words that I say to you I do not speak on My own initiative, but the Father abiding in Me does His works. (John 14:9–10)*

∽

23. There are so many different denominations calling themselves Christian, it is confusing to know if they are teaching truth or not. Which Christian convictions do you believe are not negotiable?

That is a very good question. My husband has often said that most Christian denominations agree on 95 percent of doctrinal issues and quarrel over 5 percent, which seems very silly and not a good witness to the world. Different denominations usually arise from minor points of disagreement. Sometimes, though, the differences are not minor, but quite significant, and knowing the non-negotiables is important. These, I believe, are the doctrinal beliefs that all Christians need to embrace if they call themselves followers of Christ:

- There is only one God. (Deuteronomy 6:4)
- Jesus is God's only Son. He came to this world, lived a

sinless life, died as a substitute for our sins, arose from the dead on the third day, and has ascended into Heaven, where He sits on his Father's right hand making intercession for us. (John 1:1, 3:16; Romans 8:34)

- Jesus was born of a virgin, conceived by the Holy Ghost. (Luke 1:26–35)
- The Bible is the inspired Word of God and is true and complete in its entirety. (2 Timothy 3:16)
- There is only one way to get to Heaven and that is by repenting of our sins and accepting by faith that Jesus Christ has forgiven us of them. (Ephesians 2:8–9)
- There will be a real and actual Second Coming of Christ in which believers, both those alive and those dead, are raised into Heaven to live eternally with God. (Titus 2:13)
- There will be a judgment of our lives. Those who have not accepted Christ are thrown into Hell for everlasting punishment, while those whose sins are forgiven will live for all eternity with God in Heaven. (Revelation 20:11–15)

∾ *As the deer pants for the water brooks, so my soul pants for You, O God. (Psalms 42:1)*
∾ *As I urged you upon my departure for Macedonia, remain in Ephesus so that you may instruct certain men not to teach strange doctrines. (1 Timothy 1:3)*

~

24. What differentiates a cult from a mainline denomination?

*B*asically, a religion is determined a cult if it transgresses the two foundational teachings of Christianity, which are using another authority than the Bible and believing there is another way to get to Heaven other than (or besides) the atoning blood of Jesus Christ. Look for these two pivotal teachings whenever you speak with people about their beliefs. When they are raised, you will know they believe heresy.

This truth is demonstrated by something you learned in elementary physics: If any part of an equation is wrong, then all of the answers from it are wrong. Therefore, if a religion teaches heresy in any form, then all of the religion is in vain. If I were giving one piece of advice to anyone new to Christianity who is seeking a church, it would be to see if the pastor preaches from the Bible. If you are fed the Word of God, you will grow and prosper.

∾ *Come, let us go up to the mountain of the Lord, to the house of the God of Jacob, that He may teach us His ways, and we may walk in His paths. (Micah 4:2 AMP)*
∾ *But in vain they do worship me, teaching for doctrines the commandments of men. (Matthew 15:9 KJV)*

~

25. Can a Christian be demon-possessed?

No. When we ask Jesus into our heart, the Holy Spirit takes up residence in us and lives through us. What occurs when someone is demon-possessed is exactly what the phrase sounds like: a demon, or demons, takes total control of that person and acts out his evil through her or him. The relationship comes from within. So "demon-possessed Christian" is an oxymoron.

But Christians can be demon-oppressed. This relates to a demonic attack from outside. Satan is very good at oppressing some Christians with reminders of their past life and sin, or with worry or fear, and causing them incredible emotional distress.

In order to combat the attacks of Satan, it is very important that we put on the whole armor of God every day. For someone susceptible to demonic oppression the most important part of the armor will be the helmet of salvation. If you can visualize a helmet, you will notice that it fits down over the ears of the person wearing it. In the same way, when you consciously clothe yourself daily with the emotional knowledge that you have been saved, then you can also walk in confidence that the helmet of salvation covers your ears and will help you tune out the voice of Satan trying to harass you.

∾ *Now the Spirit of the LORD departed from Saul, and an evil spirit from the LORD terrorized him. (1 Samuel 16:14)*
∾ *Any kingdom divided against itself is laid waste; and any city or house divided against itself will not stand. (Matthew 12:25)*

∾

26. I always thought that if I followed my conscience I'd be okay. My friend says that my feelings of guilt are not always dependable. Who is right?

Our conscience speaks to us through feelings. When we do something that we know is wrong, our conscience nags at us until we make things right. But your friend is also correct, because we can train our conscience to speak incorrectly. If we consistently ignore our inner voice when we're doing something we know is wrong, eventually our conscience will be silenced. We will not experience the same hurt/sadness that we did in the past. Over time we can convince ourselves that this activity is okay because our conscience no longer makes us feel bad. What has happened is that we've deafened that voice and can no long hear it.

Interestingly, it is also possible for our inner voice to speak inaccurately. There are three false voices.

- **Satan.** He tries to condemn us over sins with which we still struggle. He feeds us guilt, whispering that we cannot possibly be forgiven, but remember that he is a liar.
- **Unrealistic standards.** Our conscience will also condemn us when we expect forgiven means perfect.
- **Social standards.** It is also possible to have guilt for enjoying an activity that is not specifically frowned on in the Bible but which is not allowed by the rules of your family or church.

However, a conscience is a God-given guide to you. Train yourself to listen closely to God's voice and read the Bible regularly to keep yourself pure.

∽ *Surely God is good to Israel, to those who are pure in heart! (Psalms 73:1)*

∽ *I also do my best to maintain always a blameless conscience both before God and before men. (Acts 24:16)*

∽

27. Do you have to pray out loud?

No. God is a spirit and He does not need for you to speak audibly for Him to hear you. A good reason to pray aloud is because it is good for you to hear what your heart is saying. Your ears will record the words, and they will encourage your spirit. When you pray out loud, Satan hears and is warned.

A good example of praying silently but having God hear you is found in 1 Samuel. Hannah was a woman who longed for a child. One day she was in the temple praying to God, entreating Him for a child. She was in such emotional distress that she couldn't even speak the words, so she moaned in desperation. A year later, though, Hannah was blessed with a child who would become the Prophet Samuel.

❧ *Let the words of my mouth and the meditation of my heart be acceptable in Your sight, O LORD, my rock and my Redeemer. (Psalms 19:14)*
❧ *The eyes of the Lord watch over those who do right, and his ears are open to their prayers. (1 Peter 3:12 NLT)*

~

28. What is sin?

Sin means "missing the mark." Sin is what separates us from God. When we are born, it is the inborn sin that we carry—a sort of spiritual DNA from our forefather, Adam—that makes us sinners. Once we reach an age that we can comprehend not only God's love but also his Holy Word, we have to make the decision as to whether we wish to ask for and receive forgiveness for our sin or continue to live our life without God.

After we become born again, the Holy Spirit and the Bible will begin to convict us of things that are not pleasing to God. Then we are faced with the decision of how to respond to the Holy Spirit's correction. Will you relinquish your sin and ask God to forgive you or will you pretend it does not matter? It is when you know that God has asked you to do something but you refuse to do it—that is sin. That deliberate sin will create a wall between you and God until you bow in obedience to Him.

❧ *If I regard iniquity in my heart, the Lord will not hear me. (Psalms 66:18 KJV)*
❧ *Therefore, to one who knows the right thing to do and does not do it, to him it is sin. (James 4:17)*

29. I am a Christian, but I am afraid to be baptized. Do I have to be baptized to go to Heaven? What is the advantage?

For an answer to this question, remember Jesus' crucifixion. Do you remember the thief who believed and asked Jesus to remember Him? What was Jesus' answer? "Today you will be with me in paradise" (Luke 23:34). So this Scripture passage demonstrates that it is not baptism that gets us into Heaven, but rather believing in Jesus as our Savior.

However, Jesus instituted two ordinances that He commanded all Christians to observe until He returns. The first was water baptism and the second was communion. He clearly states in the Scriptures that He expects Christians to be baptized (Mark 16:16; Colossians 2:12).

The reason for water baptism is because it serves as a picture to other believers and unbelievers of what happens spiritually when we accept Jesus Christ as our Savior. Being lowered into the water signifies being buried in sin, while coming up out of the water signifies being raised as a new creation in Christ.

If you are afraid, you need to admit it to God and then take a step of faith and obedience and say, "I am afraid, Jesus, but I will be obedient and trust you." I encourage you to call your pastor and make the appointment to be baptized.

 When I am afraid, I will put my trust in you. (Psalms 56:3)
 For you have not received a spirit of slavery leading to fear again. (Romans 8:15)

~

30. I am a Christian, but I still fear I will not go to Heaven when I die. Why are most Christians so sure about their eternal destiny and how can I know for sure?

*A*ssurance of our eternal destiny comes from scripture. In John 14:1-3, Jesus said, "Do not let your heart be troubled . . . in my father's house are many dwelling places . . . I go to prepare a place for you . . . and will come again and receive you to myself that where I am, there you may be also." Remind yourself that you are a Christian because of your faith in Jesus, and even though salvation is immediate, it may take time for your emotions to experience assurance of its reality. Your confidence in your salvation will grow as you read the Bible and pray. To deal with fears pray for peace and protection before going to sleep, and when doubts come, speak out loud scriptures such as the one above, or: "There is now no condemnation to those who are in Christ Jesus" (Romans 8:1).

∾ *In peace I will both lie down and sleep, for You alone, O LORD, make me to dwell in safety. (Psalms 4:8)*
∾ *The Spirit Himself testifies with our spirit that we are children of God. (Romans 8:16).*

~

31. Considering how much emphasis the Bible places on love and being kind, can you ever think of instances when it is okay to lie?

*N*o. If the Bible says it is wrong to lie, it is. Once you believe that, you will not delve into "what ifs" that will confuse or cause you to rationalize.

However, even though it is wrong to lie, it does not mean that we are always to speak the plain truth. That is not wise either. This is where discretion comes in. We need to understand that we are not obligated to give our opinion on everything. Silence is not only golden; it is worth its weight in gold if it saves a relationship.

❧ *He who guards his mouth and his tongue, guards his soul from troubles. (Proverbs 21:23)*

❧ *And the tongue is a fire, the very world of iniquity; the tongue is set among our members as that which defiles the entire body, and sets on fire the course of our life, and is set on fire by hell. (James 3:6)*

FRIENDS AND RELATIONSHIPS

1. I have a friend who is so emotionally needy I feel drained after being with her. What safeguards should I put into place?

*I*n our increasingly busy, self-absorbed age, it is hard to find time to spend with friends for relaxation, let alone needy friends. However, we are not called to follow the pattern of the world but to be an example of Christ's love. God has placed her within the sphere of your influence, so you do need to reach out to her.

First of all, set some boundaries for your time together. Whenever she is low and cannot see anything positive about her world, help her to see that dwelling on problems makes their formidability increase. Point her to Jesus Christ, who can help any situation. She may not understand that we can bring our imaginations under our control, so encourage her to think on good and positive things. You can also direct her to a professional Christian counselor who will help her with healing. Teach her how to meditate on God's Word and to learn to meditate and pray when she feels emotionally empty. Before you separate each time, pray together, affirming God's work in her life.

Enlist the help of another Christian friend. Just as two comrades will help a wounded soldier off the battlefield, sharing the burden of her care will keep you from becoming exhausted. It is a practical demonstration of Ecclesiastes, "a three-fold cord is not easily broken."

∾ *A friend loves at all times, and a brother is born for adversity. (Proverbs 17:17)*
∾ *So then, while we have opportunity, let us do good to all people, and especially to those who are of the household of the faith. (Galatians 6:10)*

2. My family lives far away, and I have a new baby. I feel over-whelmed and am wondering where could I go for help?

*Y*ou need to find a church home, and quickly. In the community of other Christians, you will find friends to substitute for your family who is far away. Your greatest help will be companions who are or have been in your same situation—moms. These women will gather you close to offer encouragement, bring meals when you are overcommitted, and baby-sit when you are stressed. A weekly Bible study will provide spiritual nourishment and no doubt mentors to give you the support you need. Run, do not walk, to the nearest Bible-teaching church, and do it now. Seek out an older woman who is raising well-behaved, happy children to be your particular encourager.

∾ *God sets the lonely in families. (Psalms 68:6 NIV)*
∾ *Likewise, teach the older women to be reverent in the way they live, not to be slanderers or addicted to much wine, but to teach what is good. Then they can train the younger women to love their husbands and children, to be self-controlled and pure, to be busy at home, to be kind, and to be subject to their husbands, so that no one will malign the word of God. (Titus 2:3–5 NIV)*

~

3. I am a career woman who is single. Since my sex life will not hurt anyone, celibacy cannot be that important, can it?

A large part of being a Christian is about obedience. No matter what society leads us to believe, sex is not an entitlement, and the foundational reason not to have sex outside of marriage is because God says *no*. The biblical terms *fornication* and *sexual immorality* refer to all sexual activity outside of marriage. Leviticus, chapters 18 and 20; 1 Thessalonians, chapter 4, verse 3; and 1 Corinthians, chapter 6, verse 18, are examples of Scripture that speak to the importance of sexual purity. You are incorrect in believing that your sex life will not hurt anyone. Primarily it harms you, because everything we do affects our spirit. Furthermore, our actions influence others. John Donne said, "No man is an island entire of itself; every man is a piece of the continent, a part of the main." Your value system speaks to coworkers, neighbors, and friends.

I understand that you are seeking a relationship, but when you engage in intercourse outside of marriage, you short-change your chances for a stable one. Like a wheel within a wheel, contravening God's law damages our spirit and results in our human relationships being diminished. Sex involves such powerful emotions; it brings all other aspects of a relationship to standstill. Instead of building on shared interests and compatibility, our concentration on the physical makes our relationship shallow and unbalanced.

∾ *To obey is better than sacrifice. (1 Samuel 15:22)*
∾ *It is God's will that you should be sanctified: that you should avoid sexual immorality; that each of you should learn to control his own body in a way that is holy and honorable, not in passionate lust like the heathen, who do not know God. (1 Thessalonians 4:3–4 NIV)*

⌒

4. We just moved to a new community and I do not know anyone. How can I build relationships?

The best step you can take is to join a church. There you will find spiritual sisters who will provide lifelong support to you. A church family is often closer than our blood relatives because of the spiritual dynamics and proximity. Joining a church is the greatest gift you can give yourself. In one place you will get friends to enjoy socially, teaching for spiritual maturity, and emotional support.

Become involved in the church and avail yourself of the women's classes, such as the weekly Bible study. In a perfect world you would not have to be the first one to make a move because all the people already established would realize it is their responsibility to welcome you and help you adjust. However, if you sit back and wait for them, it may be a year or longer before you begin any relationships.

∾ *A man who has friends must himself be friendly. (Proverbs 18:24 NKJV)*
∾ *And when he wanted to go across to Achaia, the brethren encouraged him and wrote to the disciples to welcome him; and when he had arrived, he greatly helped those who had believed through grace. (Acts 18:27)*

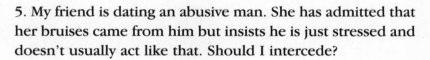

5. My friend is dating an abusive man. She has admitted that her bruises came from him but insists he is just stressed and doesn't usually act like that. Should I intercede?

You know your friend is probably living in denial, but you are not going to get her to admit it by confronting her. However, I believe that the risk of damage to your friendship is worth a try; so, pray for wisdom and look for an opportunity to ask her nonjudgmental questions. You could ask her what draws her to him. You may be able to help her see that perhaps poor self-esteem has contributed to her dependency on him. Maybe if she came from an abusive home, she may understand that she is following a generational pattern that is destructive. Additionally, look around for an older person she respects who could talk to her. Sometimes we will not take advice from contemporaries on sensitive issues but may be willing to listen to someone older whom we respect. Furthermore, because we are called to be defenders of the defenseless, as indicated in Psalms, chapter 82, verse 3, if he ever becomes abusive when you are around, call 911 and report it. Remember to cover everything with a blanket of prayer, because the power an abuser holds over another is really a spiritual bondage. Prayer has the ability to open closed minds and turn what may seem to be a hopeless situation into an acceptable resolution.

∾ *Do not associate with a man given to anger; or go with a hot-tempered man. (Proverbs 22:24)*
∾ *Brethren, even if anyone is caught in any trespass, you who are spiritual, restore such a one in a spirit of gentleness. (Galatians 6:1)*

∼

6. I am a twenty-year-old girl living away from home for the first time. In my college dorm, all the girls go out drinking every Friday night. I am lonely and tired of sitting home alone. If I do not participate in their activities, isn't it okay for me to accompany them?

*I*f you would go out with your friends, I do not imagine you would have any fun. You would probably be perplexed as to why they find enjoyment in such an empty pursuit. Instead, face that your loneliness is making you vulnerable and take some positive action.

Go to your student center and ask about the Christian sororities on your campus. Groups such as Chi Alpha and InterVarsity Christian Fellowship provide late-night weekend fun for young adults. In their company you will find coeds with your value system and have a more enjoyable time. Attend your church's college-age classes or learn a new hobby that has intrigued you for some time. Maybe there is a worthwhile cause such as the Boys & Girls Club for which you can become a faithful volunteer.

∾ *Young man, it's wonderful to be young! Enjoy every minute of it. Do everything you want to do; take it all in. But remember that you must give an account to God for everything you do. (Ecclesiastes 11:9 NLT)*
∾ *Do not participate in the unfruitful deeds of darkness. (Ephesians 5:11)*

~

7. A friend has asked for a loan of several thousand dollars. As a single career woman, I can afford it, but should I do it?

The Bible always directs us to be openhanded to those who are needy; however, the book of Proverbs also speaks about being prudent with your money. You do not say whether she is requesting the loan out of need, for a business venture, or for something she desires but cannot afford. However, the biblical guidelines regarding lending say that it is better to give a gift of the money than to loan it. One reason for this is that it will strain your friendship if she is unable to pay it back. If you can afford to make her a gift, and feel God would approve, then I would do it.

∾ *The rich rules over the poor, and the borrower becomes the lender's slave. (Proverbs 22:7)*
∾ *Treat others the same way you want them to treat you. (Luke 6:31)*

8. My friend is engaged to a man she has known less than six months. Do I have any responsibility to try and dissuade her from her decision?

*T*he ability to make wise decisions does not come easily. I can see why you are concerned about your friend. If your relationship is solid enough for you to ask her some questions, I would ask her why they feel compelled to move toward marriage at this time. Do you know how her family feels about him or how his family feels about her? Without judging, pose these and other questions that the flurry of romance might have kept out of her head. Sometimes if we do not feel driven to defend our decisions, we are more likely to re-examine them honestly.

Do not forget the power of prayer. Wrong, foolish, or ill-timed plans can be thwarted by prayer. You will probably do more to keep your relationship with your friend intact if you do your fighting on your knees instead of with your speech. If indeed she decides to marry him, enter into the plans with enthusiasm and support her wholeheartedly, now and later.

∾ *Also it is not good for a person to be without knowledge, and he who hurries his footsteps errs. (Proverbs 19:2)*
∾ *The effective prayer of a righteous man can accomplish much. (James 5:16)*

9. My friend is engaged to a man her parents dislike. Why don't they understand she is old enough to make her own choice?

*I*t isn't that they do not understand she is old enough to make her own choice but that as her parents, they realize their responsibility to offer another perspective. They may be hoping to avert what they perceive to be an unwise decision with lifelong consequences. Maturity brings life wisdom that sees things younger people may not.

In the world's philosophy, when you reach the age of legal accountability you also become totally independent. However, that may be a contributing reason some young adults falter emotionally and spiritually when they get out on their own. God's Word does not teach that we ever reach an age where we can slough off the voices of our parents or other people of influence in our lives. Even adults need to seek out older people to listen to and factor in their wisdom before reaching a decision. Our parents have seen and experienced much, and what they have learned can be usefully applied to our lives in order to avoid pitfalls.

∾ *Fools think they need no advice, but the wise listen to others. (Proverbs 12:15 NLT)*
∾ *Honor your father and mother (which is the First Commandment with a promise). (Ephesians 6:2)*

10. I have a friend who is always offended when she discovers I've done something without her—for example, if I've gone shopping with someone else. Am I a bad friend?

*I*t sounds like your friend struggles with jealousy and may be trying to control your friendship. Your friend is seeking people (you) to fill the void that only God can fill in her life. First of all, realize that she may never change. Therefore, in order for you to continue to enjoy having her as a friend, you will have to set boundaries. Continue to see other people when you wish. When she inquires about the outing in a friendly way, respond to her in like manner. However, if she is offended that she was not included, do not feel that you need to apologize or defend yourself. When she realizes that she cannot make you feel guilty, she will probably do one of two things: find another friend whom she can control or change her behavior. We'll hope she will choose the second. Pray for her and do what you can to encourage her to grow spiritually.

❧ *Jealousy is cruel as the grave. (Song of Solomon 8:6 KJV)*
❧ *For where jealousy and selfish ambition exist, there is disorder and every evil thing. (James 3:16)*

~

11. My husband and I had a very bad fight a few weeks ago and I confided in a close friend. Since then I've had three phone calls from different acquaintances that have made me aware that my friend didn't kept quiet about my confidence. I am bitter and want nothing to do with her. Should I confront her?

*Y*es, an issue left unresolved will only get worse. Even if you had not asked her not to tell anyone, a basic tenet of friendship is that confidences do not go any farther than the person they are repeated to. Before you speak to her, rehearse what you are going to say and pray about your response to her. How will you react if she gets defensive? What will you say if she denies saying anything to anyone? Above all, what do you want the end result to be? Are you willing to forego a close friendship because of one slip-up?

As painful as her action is, the damage that is done will continue to erode your spirit until you forgive her. Remember that forgiveness is a voluntary act in which our emotions sometimes take a while to reflect our decision. In other words, after you forgive her you may still not feel forgiving toward her, so you will have to disregard your feelings and concentrate on what you did. Pray for her. Ask God to give you a heart of forgiveness. Deliberately act toward her as if there has been no hurt.

Finally, do not consider the experience wasted. You have learned the truth of that old homily that says two people can keep a secret as long as one of them is dead. Do not trust someone with information that you do not want to be passed along. Sometimes people blurt out information without even being aware that they should not have done so. I know that has been my response to life; I like to get the words out there so I can examine them along with everybody else, but that sometimes leads to a big "oops."

↬ *A gossip betrays a confidence, but a trustworthy man keeps a secret. (Proverbs 11:13 NIV)*
↬ *For if ye forgive men their trespasses, your Heavenly Father will also forgive you. (Matthew 6:14 KVJ)*

~

12. A friend and I were involved in an accident. She asked me to say I was driving, even though she had been, as she had left her purse at home. I said *no,* and now she is angry at me for not being a true friend. Should I have done what she asked?

*Y*ou did the right thing. First of all, it was dishonest, and, second, it was something she should never have asked of you. You are right to understand that there are boundaries in any relationship that should not be crossed. True friends say things that are hard because they are truly concerned for the integrity of their relationship. Continue to go out of your way to call and invite her out with you, because as she cools down, she will probably be embarrassed at what she asked you to do in the heat of the moment.

41

∾ *Who may ascend into the hill of the LORD? And who may stand in His holy place? He who has clean hands and a pure heart, who does not lift up his soul to an idol or swear by what is false. (Psalms 24:3–4)*

∾ *Keep a clear conscience, so that those who speak maliciously against your good behavior in Christ may be ashamed of their slander. (1 Peter 3:16 NIV)*

~

13. In our circle of friends, there is someone who is oil to my water. We never agree. How can I make peace with this person?

Conflict is inevitable. It began in the Garden of Eden and has continued to today. Since there will always be disagreements, it is important to learn Christ's strategy for dealing with conflict. The first is to adopt the mind of Christ by not involving ourselves in senseless arguing. When accused of something, our best response often is to keep silent. Second, it is best to learn to submit to the person we have a conflict with by paying attention to her or his needs first. A universal principle of Christian life is to yield our desires to another's. Finally, we need to aspire for peace with others by being peaceable ourselves.

You do not have to like everyone, but you do have to love them. Ask God to give you insight into their hearts that you may have a better understanding of them. Remember to extend to them the same grace God has extended to you. Finally, consider the fact that maybe God has brought that person into your life to do some work on yourself. We are all a work in progress.

∾ *Iron sharpens iron; so one man sharpens another. (Proverbs 27:17)*

❧ *If possible, so far as it depends on you, be at peace with all men. (Romans 12:18)*

~

14. My friend insists that anyone who goes into marriage without living together first is just asking for a divorce because they haven't worked out the issues beforehand. Could she be right?

*Y*our friend is simply giving out popular advice that is someone's opinion and not grounded in truth. If we are wise, we will build relationships on biblical values that have stood for all time, not current trends. Next time she brings it up, you can dispute her arguments with these facts: A recent study by the Center for Marital and Family Studies at the University of Denver, as reported in the *Idaho Statesman* newspaper (July 13, 2002), found that "men who want 'to test marriage out first' are less committed to the institution in general and their partners specifically, than men who move directly to marriage without cohabitating," and "ironically, the divorce rate among those who once lived together is higher than among those who have not." (Even more ironic is that these findings line up with scriptural precepts written almost 2,000 years ago.) It seems that commitment is the key to a long-lasting relationship and "trying it out first" lacks that essential ingredient.

❧ *How blessed is the man who does not walk in the counsel of the wicked, nor stand in the path of sinners, nor sit in the seat of scoffers! But his delight is in the law of the LORD, and in His law he meditates day and night. (Psalms 1:1–2)*
❧ *Marriage is to be held in honor among all, and the marriage bed is to be undefiled. (Hebrews 13:4)*

15. The neighbor's teenage son backed out of their driveway and hit my parked car. I've spoken to the father, but while they agree their son is at fault, he does not have a job, so he can't pay us. As the father said, "You have insurance, don't you?" Should I sue him?

So often the legal choice may not be the wise one. Yes, your neighbor should have offered to pay; but his information may be correct, so check with your insurance company. Many policies have provisions for just these instances; they are called "Good Neighbor" clauses because insurance companies understand that it is very hard to sue a neighbor, friend, or family member who inflicts damage on your property.

Is this the first time your neighbor has caused harm to your property? Can you calmly suggest that while you do not intend to sue, the son probably should be made to accept responsibility for his actions and could he do yard work for you to pay for it? This no doubt involves going the extra mile, but I believe you would not feel good about bringing charges against someone in such close proximity to you, because the bad feelings it may engender are not worth it.

On a practical note, even if you take them to small-claims court and win, how are you going to collect? They could still refuse to pay, and this after all kinds of bad communications will have been aired. Suing does not augur well for future relationships.

Finally, there is the principle of turning the other cheek. No one says you have to fight this battle. Sometimes the best course is to simply let it pass. Remember you are not responsible for their son. You do not have to pursue this.

∾ *The beginning of strife is like letting out water, so abandon the quarrel before it breaks out. (Proverbs 17:14)*
∾ *Settle matters quickly with your adversary. (Matthew 5:25 NIV)*

16. My husband and I, both believers, are considering an offer from friends to become partners in their grocery business. They are very ethical people, and our values line up, so we wonder if the fact that they are unbelievers should weigh in our decision?

*W*hile I believe that your friends are ethical people, it is doubtful that you have the same values. When hard times come (which they have a habit of doing in today's business world), the decisions that will be made under stress, and the urgency to profit, may not continue to be similar. The parameters of your code of ethics are set by Scripture, while in the matter of business even moral people often rationalize their ethics when it comes to the profit line in their company. Your partners will not bring the spiritual power that is not only necessary for guidance in your business decisions, but will also be a support during the company's sure-to-happen downtimes.

That being said, I cannot insist that Scripture disapproves of business partnerships between believers and unbelievers. To insist on this practice would mean we would also only buy and sell to the Christian community (and subsequently go broke). However, if you have prayed earnestly about your decision and in your prayers not felt God telling you not to do it, then I would proceed with it. I would encourage you be very open about any areas you may have concerns about, even going so far as to having the parameters of these issues written into the contract.

Finally, I believe you will certainly be a blessing to your friends if you choose to become business partners. Scripture has many instances that demonstrate the blessing that godly workers bring to the businesses that employ them.

∾ *In all your ways acknowledge him and he will direct your paths. (Proverbs 3:6)*
∾ *But if any of you lacks wisdom, let him ask of God, who*

gives to all generously and without reproach, and it will be given to him. (James 1:5)

~

17. My parents are quite elderly and soon we'll be faced with the decision of what to do when they can no longer care for themselves. Is there a biblical standard as to my responsibility to have them in my home, or does God approve of nursing homes?

*R*emember, the people of the Bible did not have a choice as to who cared for their elderly. Nursing homes are an advent of our modern society. There is no one-size-fits-all answer to this situation. Each family is different, and what is best for my parents may not be what is best for yours. So, there isn't any biblical absolute. Just remember the principle that we are to honor and care for our parents. The best way to honor them is to give credence to their opinions regarding where and how they are cared for.

∾ *You shall rise up before the gray headed and honor the aged. (Leviticus 19:32)*
∾ *Honor your father and mother (which is the First Commandment with a promise). (Ephesians 6:2)*

~

18. My high school son's best friend has recently become born again. His parents are very disapproving of religion and have barred him from going to church. He has been sneaking out on Sunday mornings anyway. I am not sure if I should be proud of him for standing up for his beliefs, or if I am encouraging his rebellion.

I sincerely hope you are not encouraging his duplicity. It is easy for zealousness to overcome wisdom, but he needs to be confronted. As a high school student, he is under his parents' authority and you must honor them. Help him understand his parents' view: They may know nothing about Christianity or have a negative view of Christians, for Christians do not always have a shining reputation. Maybe they are worried that he has fallen in with a cult. Explain to him that if he can demonstrate in his home (the very hardest place to witness) that Jesus Christ has changed his life, his parents may change their minds about letting him attend church.

He is not the first person to serve God in unfriendly situations. In the book of Daniel, Daniel and his three friends were asked to do something contrary to God's laws. They respectfully offered an alternative to the commands and the rulers granted it. In the same way, your son's friend may make an appeal to his parents for permission to attend church once a week. If his attitude is correct, they just may grant it. If it seems appropriate, you can offer to go with him to speak to them.

Stress to him that the fact he is a Christian does not come from attending church. As important as church attendance is, when it is impossible to join with believers, God will extend extra grace to him.

Your responsibility is to sustain him spiritually. Support him with lots of prayer. Make his spiritual survival a project within your church, bringing them regular reports so they will know how to pray for him. Supply him with a good teen-version Bible, music, and books to read. Do not let your contact fall away.

❧ My son, observe the commandment of your father and do not forsake the teaching of your mother. (Proverbs 6:20)
❧ Children, obey your parents in the Lord, for this is right. (Ephesians 6:1)

19. I happen to know as a fact that one of the elders in our church is having an affair. Do I have any right or obligation to confront him about this?

*M*any people are surprised to discover that there are guidelines in the Bible for resolving interpersonal problems. The most important consideration is that you are very sure of your facts. You are not to do anything if it is speculation. Then, following the guidelines in Matthew (18:15–17), you need first to confront him yourself. If he immediately repents of his sin and abandons the behavior, you have rescued a soul. However, if he does not confess his sin or admit that he is sinning, you are to go with another witness and confront him. Should this not bring repentance, then you are to go before the church, where if he still does not repent, he is to be asked to leave the fellowship.

ɶ *Who will confront him with his actions, and who will repay him for what he has done? (Job 21:31)*
ɶ *An overseer, then, must be above reproach, the husband of one wife, temperate, prudent, respectable, hospitable, able to teach. (1 Timothy 3:2)*

~

20. My roommate casually "grazes" in the produce department each week while we do our grocery shopping. She insists it is not stealing, as stores expect their customers to sample it before buying it.

I imagine she honestly believes what she is saying. However, the Eighth Commandment clearly says "thou shalt not steal." If there isn't a sign that invites us to sample, we are left having to accept that we are taking property that is not ours, which does make it stealing.

Your best solution may be to divide up the grocery list so you are going to different parts of the store, meeting back at the checkout to pay.

᛫ *You shall not steal. (Exodus 20:15)*
᛫ *He who steals must steal no longer. (Ephesians 4:28)*

~

21. A deacon in our church recently spent $25,000 on his daughter's wedding. Isn't this a shameful waste of money when so many people go to bed hungry each night?

*I*t is perfectly okay for you to decide that you will not spend that amount of money on your daughter's wedding, but what someone else chooses to do with his money is between him and God. In the Gospels some people complained about a woman using a jar of costly perfume to anoint Jesus' feet, saying that the money would have been better spent to feed the poor. However, Jesus rebuked their attitude. In the same way, do not bother yourself over someone else's actions that do not affect you, but concentrate on doing what God has told you to do.

I also hope you are not verbalizing your "concerns" to anyone else, because that would be gossip, which the Bible does consider shameful.

᛫ *Therefore do not associate with a gossip. (Proverbs 20:19)*
᛫ *They have become filled with every kind of wickedness, evil, greed and depravity. They are full of envy, murder, strife, deceit and malice. They are gossips. (Romans 1:29 NIV)*

22. How can I encourage my boyfriend spiritually?

*O*ne way you can encourage your boyfriend is, with his permission, hold him accountable for his Christian walk. Probably one of the greatest tools for spiritual growth is accountability. Ask him in what areas he would like you to hold him accountable. Some suggestions would be to ask him if he is having regular devotions; what God has been speaking to him about recently; what books he is reading and movies he is watching.

Also, evaluate what signals your actions or manner of dress may give to him. We do not live in a vacuum, and revealing clothing and provocative behavior on your part will be a hindrance to his desire to be spiritually pure.

∾ *And Jonathan, Saul's son, arose and went to David at Horesh, and encouraged him in God. (1 Samuel 23:16)*
∾ *He rejoiced and began to encourage them all with resolute heart to remain true to the Lord. (Acts 11:23)*

~

23. I am in a position that I never thought I would be. Members of my college/career group at church were recently talking about their favorite movies. I was shocked at what movies they consider to be their favorites. Many of them were R-rated. Some of them I had seen when I was an unbeliever, but not the more recent ones because I did not consider them appropriate for Christians. Am I being odd over this issue?

*N*o. Differences in standards are quite common among Christians. What appears to be a black-and-white issue to one may appear to be a matter of individual conscience to another. Do not judge them for what they consider acceptable for viewing, but neither should you violate the standard that the Holy Spirit has asked of you. Sometimes Christians fall prey to the "everyone is doing it" prevailing train of thought. If no one raises the standard, they are not aware of the compromises they are making. Your witness will do one of two things: make them mad because they do not want to be made to feel that their decisions are not pleasing to God, or it will challenge their hearts to re-examine their life standards.

∾ *I will set no worthless thing before my eyes. (Psalms 101:3)*
∾ *I pray that the eyes of your heart may be enlightened. (Ephesians 1:18)*

24. I am a married woman in my mid-twenties. Recently a close friend who is single confided that she has signed up with a Christian dating service in hopes of finding a Christian husband. I am appalled and worried that she would be so desperate. Do I have a wrong perspective on her actions?

I do not believe there is anything wrong with her decision or that she is desperate. To catch fish you have to go where they are. She may not know any Christian men other than married ones and this seems a viable option.

However, since she opened the subject, be a sounding board for her. Help her examine her reasons for seeking a husband. She may discover in the process that her reasons for wishing to be married need re-examining. Be a good listener and at an appropriate time remind her that even when she finds "Mr. Perfect," the final decision needs to be set before God for approval.

Broaden her thinking and propose to her that God may have a different plan for her life than that of marriage. Help her see that this world has many options open to single women that she may wish to take advantage of before marrying.

∾ *Hope deferred makes the heart sick, but desire fulfilled is a tree of life. (Proverbs 13:12)*
∾ *I will therefore that the younger women marry, bear children, guide the house, give none occasion to the adversary to speak reproachfully. (1 Timothy 5:14 KJV)*

∼

25. My friend is very opinionated about what she considers appropriate Christian music. She says that most of the new music is really demonic because of the heavy beat and minor chords. I really like the new groups but do not want to be worshiping Satan either. How do I know if she is right or not?

I have said that the mommy war is the longest-running conflict in modern Christianity, but music styles is the second longest—and by far the hotter issue. You will not change someone's mind if they are not willing to accept that their belief in music is a preference not a mandate. When they are a visitor in your house, turn their music on (or all music off). Otherwise, worship God in the manner that blesses you and allows you the liberty to worship the most freely.

The Bible's command to make a joyful noise in praise to God does not include any qualifiers. There is nothing that says it has to be a certain tempo, beat, or major versus minor chords. My cousin who is a missionary in the Middle East shared an interesting perspective on music preferences. To people of East Indian culture, the Western world's preference for major chords appears disharmonious and ugly, while their minor chords (what we may call "wailing") are what are most appealing to them.

God leaves the style of celebration to the myriad types and cultures of people. I doubt you will ever convince your friend otherwise, and you probably should not try.

∽ *Sing for joy to God our strength; shout joyfully to the God of Jacob. (Psalms 81:1)*
∽ *Speaking to one another in psalms and hymns and spiritual songs, singing and making melody with your heart to the Lord. (Ephesians 5:19)*

∽

26. As grandmother of three beautiful children, what long-lasting gift can I give them?

You can give them the gift of prophetic prayer. By this I mean for you to pray for God's attributes and character to be developed in their lives as if it were already evident. When you pray these faith requests aloud, you are asking the Holy Spirit to partner with you for your grandchildren's spiritual growth. It will increase your faith on behalf of them.

First of all, find a Scripture that embodies a spiritual attribute you would like to see developing in their lives. Pray this Scripture aloud every day, believing that God will begin to incorporate it in their character. Any Scripture that speaks well of a person in the Bible will do, but if you are not familiar with the pattern, a good place to look for them is in the introductions and salutations of the Epistles. For example, I could pray for my son: "I pray, David, that the eyes of your heart will be enlightened so that you will know the hope to which Jesus has called you and the riches of his glorious inheritance" (Ephesians 1:18 NIV). You can pray it alone, but if you say it to them, their minds and hearts will begin to respond to the work of the Holy Spirit in their lives.

For years, as I dropped the kids off at school, I have

prayed a benediction on them: "The LORD bless you and keep you; The LORD make his face shine upon you and be gracious to you; the LORD turn his face toward you and give you peace" (Numbers 6:24 NIV).

A friend recently related to me that when she was younger and would spend a weekend with her grandparents, every night before bed they would read to her out of their devotion book and discuss with her what the Scriptures said. Her grandma and grandpa took an interest in what she was doing and how she was growing spiritually. I can attest to the lasting effect this had on her because today she is a dedicated young Christian mother raising two children to serve the Lord.

Another gift they will cherish would be the gift of time. Children today are shunted from one activity and appointment to the next. Their lives are organized, standardized, and compartmentalized with the end result often being depersonalized. To have the gift of an adult who will give them one whole day (or afternoon or evening or hour) just to listen to them is an unbelievable luxury.

A few additional ideas and/or projects for grandparents with their grandchildren are baking cookies, storytelling, sharing vacations, baby-sitting, coaching them on their memory verses for Sunday school, providing transportation to church, games, activities, being a sounding board (someone safe to go to when they feel Mom and Dad don't understand), and attending their school programs during the day when their parents are working.

∾ *A good man leaves an inheritance to his children's children. (Proverbs 13:22)*
∾ *For I am mindful of the sincere faith within you, which first dwelt in your grandmother Lois and your mother Eunice, and I am sure that it is in you as well. (2 Timothy 1:5)*

27. My friend came to me several months ago for advice about a situation. I offered her the best counsel I had, which she took. Unfortunately, that obviously wasn't the best choice, and now she's mad at me for my advice. What should I do?

*B*e honest with her and apologize for any pain that your advice caused her. Tell her that, at the time, you felt it to be the best advice; but it obviously was not. Then ask her what you can do to help her. The only bad response to a bad situation is indifference. Humbling yourself is good for your character and will, I hope, restore your relationship.

∾ *What can we say to my Lord? What can we speak? And how can we justify ourselves? (Genesis 44:16)*
∾ *You are those who justify yourselves in the sight of men, but God knows your hearts. (Luke 16:15)*

28. My child's best friend's mother was killed by the child's father during an argument. What can I do to help my seven-year-old deal with this trauma?

*O*ne of the hardest lessons for us to accept, let alone teach our children, is that bad things happen for which we cannot find any explanations. Your child needs extra amounts of love and assurance in order to deal with this trauma. One thing he will need help with will be the ever-present talk about it at school. Encourage him to bring his questions to you and role-play with him about the things he might hear on the playground regarding what happened. You can help him come up with answers and comments to give when it does.

Even if your child does not verbalize his fear that his daddy may kill his mommy, you need to address it, because it is in his mind. Assure him that you and Daddy love Jesus and him very much, and that neither of you will ever do something like that to hurt him or each other.

Focus on what your family can do to offer comfort at this time. Help him write a letter of condolence to his friend and include a small gift. Together bake something to take to the family. At night before you go to sleep, pray together for the family, the children, and the father.

Your compassion will be your best tool and will offer him practical hope for all the other situations in life that will not make sense.

~ *This is what the LORD Almighty says: "Administer true justice; show mercy and compassion to one another." (Zechariah 7:9 NIV)*

~ *Be kind and compassionate to one another. (Ephesians 4:32 NIV)*

FAMILY

1. My husband and I are facing our kids' adolescence, our midlife, and our parents' aging. How are we to cope?

First of all, focus on the truth that God is our anchor through every season of our life. Probably your greatest problem will be coping emotionally. You need to be honest with yourselves about what you can remove from your lives in order to keep from being overwhelmed. If at all possible, decline to become involved in any new responsibilities on the job or in the community. Wherever financially possible, hire help for jobs you once had time for, such as house-cleaning or lawn work, unless you find these tasks soothing. If you have never done it before, start now to make a schedule of your commitments. Divide family responsibilities between all members. Ask yourself whether purchasing another car so your kids can perform routine errands will free you. Regular exercise and spiritual renewal will keep stress from destroying your health. Above all, remember that this too shall pass.

∞ *I am attacked from all sides, but you will rescue me unharmed by the battle. (Psalms 55:18 CEV)*
∞ *Peace I leave with you, My peace I give to you; not as the world gives do I give to you. Do not let your heart be troubled, nor let it be fearful. (John 14:27)*

2. I fear my siblings and I will drift apart when our parents die. How can I guard against it?

It is a fact that we find the time for whatever we consider important. If our siblings are important to us, we will discover ways to get together. While you are busy with careers and raising a family you will find it much harder, but even then it can be done. It is important that you establish a relationship now, outside the times when your parents bring you together. I work with a friend who is one of five sisters. Each year the five women get together for their own vacation. They have gone kayaking on the Colorado River, sightseeing in Rome, been to Disneyland, and rented a cabin in the woods. This makes the two times my sisters and I have met at a sibling's house for a reunion seem like pretty dull fare. However, I'm pretty sure we had as much fun as my friend, Judy, and her sisters did. The purpose was to bond, and we did. If you live in close proximity, make a standing breakfast/lunch date once a month at a local restaurant. Invite them over to your house on occasion without including your parents. If they live far away, keep in touch often via e-mail and phone. Use your vacation time to visit them and strengthen your relationship. Building a bond now will keep your relationship flourishing after your parents are gone.

If all of your siblings are flung across the globe as happens in many families, do a group e-mail letter to them once a week. If not everyone has a computer, start a round-robin letter. You would write a letter and mail it to a brother or sister. They would read your letter, add their own, and mail both to the next sibling. It would continue in like fashion around the members of the family. When it got back to you, it would include all the letters. You would simply replace yours with a new one and send it on its way again.

Plan a conference call each week with your brothers and sisters. Set up a prearranged time—say Saturday night—and everyone can plan to be home to take part in the call. This may seem odd to a younger generation. However, there are those of us that remember sitting at home many nights during the war, waiting for a loved one to call at a preappointed time. We gladly sacrificed our schedules to speak for a few minutes to a sibling who was on leave.

Keeping close is a matter of the heart. When you love

them and wish to remain a part of their lives, you will find a creative manner in which to do it.

∾ *You are my brothers; you are my bone and my flesh. (2 Samuel 19:12)*
∾ *Keep on loving each other as brothers. (Hebrews 13:1 NIV)*

~

3. What help can I give to my sister, who is the primary caregiver for our parents because I live hundreds of miles away?

*Y*ou are correct in believing that part of your biblical responsibility toward your parents will be fulfilled by supporting your sister as caregiver to them. First of all, ask her for suggestions. If she is not able to tell you, contact an in-home health care agency and ask them for suggestions. They can tell you the areas with which your sibling will probably need the most help.

Consider giving up one week of your vacation in order to stay with your parents. This will give your sister a free week to either leave town or simply to enjoy seven days of freedom. Some other practical ideas, depending on your finances, would be to pay for once-a-week housecleaning for your sister, gift certificates to area restaurants, or a day being pampered at a spa.

When I've spoken about this to friends who are the primary caregiver for their parents, they have told me that the most important aspect of help comes from others' appreciation for what they are doing. When you verbalize your admiration, it validates your sister's efforts. You also need to be a sounding board regarding the decisions she is facing, but do not insist on your choice. You are not the one facing the circumstances each day, and she needs permission to do what she feels is best.

ை *A wise son makes a father glad, but a foolish son is a grief to his mother. (Proverbs 10:1)*

ை *But whoever has the world's goods, and beholds his brother in need and closes his heart against him, how does the love of God abide in him? (1 John 3:17)*

~

4. My father has always been abusive. Now that I am an adult, I do not wish to have anything to do with him. That is okay, isn't it?

You may feel your decision is justified, but I imagine that you are still in pain. You have probably already discovered that distancing yourself physically has not solved the problem. Truthfully, the relationship really isn't the issue here. You may be surprised to discover that the real issue here is forgiveness. When we are unforgiving, the noxious weed of bitterness grows and it will eventually destroy us. The way to free yourself from your father's ability to continue to inflict pain on you is to forgive him. When you forgive, you will be set free and enable yourself to begin the process of healing.

However, forgiving your father does not mean you have to allow him full access to your life. You can set the boundaries and the time limit. Be realistic about the forgiving process, because that is what it is. Your mind may be set on forgiveness, but your emotions will take a while to come around. One good practice is to take stock of your self-talk. Examine the language that goes on in your mind whenever you contemplate your dad. Your thinking will probably need to be adjusted. The biblical principal of forgiveness, interestingly, is not for the good of the person who has wronged you. Primarily, it is for healing you. See the bibliography for some recommended reading on this subject.

∾ A joyful heart is good medicine, but a broken spirit dries up the bones. (Proverbs 17:22)
∾ Don't repay evil for evil. Don't retaliate when people say unkind things about you. Instead, pay them back with a blessing. (1 Peter 3:8 NLT)

∾

5. How can I help two family members (who claim to be Christians) resolve their conflicts and gain peace with each other? Both parties feel they are totally right. They each feel they have taken all the right steps to reconciliation and the other has not.

There is an important principle in Scripture regarding this: not everything that occurs in your area of influence is your responsibility. First of all, do not take part in their feud. If you plan a social event, do not allow one to blackmail you by saying, "If she's coming, I am not." If that happens, say that you will really miss seeing him/her and hope he or she will reconsider. Second, do not listen to either side's complaints about the other, for that is taking part in gossip.

However, do not discount the possibility that God may open a door for you to speak scriptural truths into their lives. Maybe they do not understand that we are always to offer forgiveness or seek peace whenever possible. Maybe they have never heard that offenses aren't offensive if we choose not to let them disturb us. While not addressing specific situations, you can point out scriptural truths such as these to help them mature.

∾ Like one who takes a dog by the ears is he who passes by and meddles with strife not belonging to him. (Proverbs 26:17)

◦ *This you know, my beloved brethren. But everyone must be quick to hear, slow to speak and slow to anger. (James 1:19)*

～

6. **A cousin of mine will be getting out of prison in six months and coming to live in our hometown. His imprisonment resulted from molesting my ten-year-old. I come from a very close family and am already dreading the next family get-together. What am I going to do?**

*G*od's heart is toward the helpless, especially children. Extending forgiveness does not include placing children back in harm's way. I hope you are working on forgiving him and helping your child to do so; but you should not feel obligated to allow him access to your child. First, communicate to your family that you will not be attending family gatherings at which he will be present. I hope you will not meet with opposition, but if it comes, do not be deterred from your position or become involved in arguments about it.

Second, check the laws in your state. In many of them a sex offender is not allowed to be in gatherings in which children are present. That is why some churches now offer adult-only services for ex-offenders.

I would also encourage you to be honest with your child. She needs to be told that this man is being released from prison, as it would cause her more harm to accidentally meet him in a public place at some time. Assure her that you will protect her and not allow him within her vicinity. She needs that security.

◦ *Vengeance is mine, and retribution, in due time their foot will slip; for the day of their calamity is near, and the impending things are hastening upon them. (Deuteronomy 32:35)*
◦ *But whoever causes one of these little ones who believe in*

Me to stumble, it would be better for him to have a heavy mill-stone hung around his neck, and to be drowned in the depth of the sea. (Matthew 18:6)

~

7. My older brother has insinuated himself into my parents' good graces. He is on their checkbook and house title. I am afraid he will get everything when they die.

I think your problem is jealousy and, maybe, greed. Your parents have the right to leave their possessions to anyone they wish, including your brother. If you do not fully accept this, then if what you fear happens, it will keep you from having a much-needed relationship with him after their deaths. I do not see that your fears have any evidence to support them. He is probably on their checkbook for practical reasons—just as siblings of mine are on our parents' bank account. Maybe they travel during the cold winter months and he takes care of the routine bills and upkeep that occur.

Your worry over unsubstantiated fears is destroying your peace of mind and maybe your health. Much of what we stress about never comes to pass. You would be better served to continue to build a strong relationship with your family and not worry about material possessions.

You did not say if he has been the one who has been there for them all through the years. Perhaps you have lived elsewhere or been busy with other responsibilities. If so, that may also have something to do with it.

∾ *For anger slays the foolish man, and jealousy kills the simple. (Job 5:2)*
∾ *Let us not become boastful, challenging one another, envying one another. (Galatians 5:26)*

64

8. Growing up, my parents showed favoritism to my sister. They have been dead five years, and I am still angry. Because of my bad feelings, I do not have a relationship with her.

*Y*our anger and jealousy seem to have eaten away at your whole life. Ask God to cleanse your heart of the bitterness you have carried and to give you a new view of her. Call your sister and invite her to go out to lunch with you. Because you are beginning to face your feelings and have not worked out what is true or untrue, at this time keep your negative feelings to yourself and the conversation on topics other than family wherever possible.

Someday He may open an opportunity for you to talk with her about your feelings. Do so in a nonblaming manner. You may be surprised at her perspective. Usually, when we are eaten up by jealousy, the other party is totally unaware that it is happening. An even crazier possibility is that she may have felt that you were the one who got special treatment. Our perspectives on childhood situations are not always reliable.

You have been forfeiting a wonderful relationship all of your life because it seems to me you have not been mature in your thinking patterns. Please do not allow resentment to control your life any longer.

❧ *Please let there be no strife between you and me . . . for we are brothers. (Genesis 13:8)*
❧ *For where envying and strife is, there is confusion and every evil work. (James 3:16 KJV)*

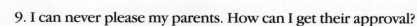

9. I can never please my parents. How can I get their approval?

*F*irst of all you need to explore the fact that sometimes the way we feel may not be accurate. Emotions can be misinterpreted and feelings are not the most reliable measure of reality. It may be possible that you and your parents did not communicate well, but that would not mean that they did not approve of you. For the sake of discussion though, let us say that you do have a dysfunctional relationship and that they have always disapproved of you. That does not make you a bad or insignificant person. Everyone needs to come to terms with the fact that they may not measure up to someone else's expectations. Seeking approval from people is the wrong focus. It is inhibiting. The only person's approval you need is God's and your own. When you realize how much God loves you and how valuable you are in His sight, your self-esteem will rise.

Being free of people's expectations is very freeing emotionally. Interestingly, when we become a confident person, others don't find it so easy to find fault with us. Plus, when criticism is given, it will not have the power to hurt us easily.

❧ *Even if my father and mother abandon me, the LORD will hold me close. (Psalms 27:10 NLT)*
❧ *I am not trying to please people. I want to please God. Do you think I am trying to please people? If I were doing that, I would not be a servant of Christ. (Galatians 1:10 CEV)*

~

10. All of my husband's family smoke and drink. We do not allow either of these activities in our home, nor do we want our children to indulge in these practices when they grow up. Now the family refuses to come to our house because of our rules. Is there a solution I am overlooking?

You might need to assess your priorities. What is more important—that your kids never associate with smokers and drinkers or for them to enjoy the blessings of an extended family? When put down this plainly, I hope you see how your reasoning may appear to others. There are solutions available. Smoking is a very tenacious addiction, and they may not be able to go several hours without a cigarette. Therefore, plan to entertain outdoors where it will not be such a point of contention. As for alcohol, I do not imagine any guest would insist on bringing his own bottle uninvited to your home. I have never had a family member get up and leave because I did not serve wine at dinner. I doubt that you will either.

I am left believing that the real point of contention may be your self-righteous indignation over habits you consider unclean. Is it possible that it is your attitude they resent? Could you re-examine the comments and behaviors you have exhibited toward them? These may be contributing to the schism. Remember, Christ dined with the lowest of society. He was even called a drunkard simply because he associated with drinkers. I encourage you to demonstrate more grace toward your family.

๛ *A gracious woman attains honor. (Proverbs 11:16)*
๛ *If I speak with the tongues of men and of angels, but do not have love, I have become a noisy gong or a clanging cymbal. (1 Corinthians 13:1)*

~

11. I cringe every time I hear a minister say that God wishes to relate to us like a father. Since my father was very abusive, how do I change my image of God?

It is true that God desires a nurturing relationship with us, such as what those with a strong parent-child bond enjoy. Many Scriptures give word pictures of Him cradling us to his breast like a mother and giving us good gifts like a father.

However, you are not alone in your reaction, as many adults suffer the same hesitation that you do. They struggle a long time reconciling to the idea that God is their father and a loving God. Isn't it nice to know that God's Word is truth? In the Scriptures you will find God to be the ultimate, perfect father figure you have been seeking all your life. Unlike humans (with their failures), God will never fail you. He will never harm you. He is always on your side rooting for your success and ever watchful about your care. Instead of struggling to reconcile the two different examples, concentrate instead on the truth about God that is revealed in Scripture. (See the bibliography for recommended books on this issue.)

∾ *A father of the fatherless, and a judge for the widows, is God in His holy habitation. (Psalms 68:5)*
∾ *If you then, being evil, know how to give good gifts to your children, how much more will your Father who is in Heaven give what is good to those who ask Him! (Matthew 7:11)*

∼

12. One of my cousins, a born-again Christian, suffered from a chemical imbalance all his life. He committed suicide last week. Is it possible that he will still go to Heaven?

I hope you understand that this is a question I cannot answer as an absolute. However, I do believe that there are principles that may help you find peace. It is so easy to categorize sin and say, "Well, suicide is murder and murder is a sin, and no sinner will enter Heaven, so he must not have gone to Heaven." The trouble with such reasoning is that I keep coming back to God's grace. None of us can live perfect lives. We all depend on His grace when we fail.

A second false assumption of many is that legitimate sickness can only occur in the body from the neck down, never the neck up. In other words, mental illness is controllable if you would only try harder. That is not true. Our minds can undergo just as real a break as an arm would if you fell out of a tree. A chemical imbalance such as a bipolar disorder is a genuine and terrifying illness.

Finally, it is not God's nature to judge someone for something beyond his or her control. If your cousin was not cognizant of what he was doing, then you can depend on God's grace. If he loved God, had asked Jesus to come into his life, and was committed to serving God within all his capabilities, I have no hesitation in saying, "Yes, you will meet him again in Heaven." And this time, he will be well!

∾ *He was wounded for our transgressions, he was bruised for our iniquities: the chastisement of our peace was upon him; and with his stripes we are healed. (Isaiah 53:5 KJV)*
∾ *Which is easier, to say, "Your sins have been forgiven you," or to say, "Get up and walk"? (Luke 5:23)*

∾

13. Do family traditions serve any purpose? If so, how do I start them?

I believe that celebrations are very important to God. Why else did He institute so many of them for His people? His celebrations are full of food, pageantry, and tradition. Traditions serve to create wonderful memories in the lives of children. They provide a thread which future generations can grasp to attain identity with family who are no longer alive. To begin traditions, simply find something that your family likes to do and continue to do it regularly or during the customary seasons of the year. It can be camping, bungee jumping, or playing Tiddlywinks.

For the past several years, we have rented a house on the

Oregon coast over Labor Day with another family in our church whose children are the same age as ours. We spend the days on the beach crafting a wonderful sandcastle surrounded by an impregnable moat. When the tide comes in and washes it away, we retreat to the house to plan an even more formidable sand structure for the next low tide. We play games, watch videos, and continue our quest to visit each lighthouse still in existence on the Oregon coast. Each member anticipates it through the summer months and reminisces about it during the winter. By sharing expenses, it is an affordable special time our children will always remember.

Holidays easily lend themselves to tradition, so use them to establish meaningful times. Open your presents the same time each year in the same manner, serve the same special menu, and rewatch *It's a Wonderful Life.* Celebrate important family days in the same way. You can buy a simple china plate at the dollar store and use paint to decorate it as an "I Am Special" plate for the person who has done something memorable to eat off for a day. And memorable can have any meaning you choose: birthdays, potty training, or a good report card. It does not matter how you celebrate, it just matters that you do.

∾ *The lines have fallen to me in pleasant places; Indeed, my heritage is beautiful to me. (Psalms 16:6)*
∾ *Hold to the traditions which you were taught. (2 Thessalonians 2:15)*

∾

14. The spouses of our two children do not get along. What can I do about the tension at family gatherings?

*I*f what you say is true, there is no sense pretending it is not happening. The Bible says in Matthew, chapter 5, verse 9, "Blessed are the peacemakers." So the next time the family gets together, address all of them by saying, "I notice that we do not seem to enjoy ourselves as one family. What can we do about it?" In this way you are not singling out the in-laws who you believe are at the cause of the stress. If your question doesn't open honest communication, it may at least bring them to the realization that they need to reassess their manners. Keep the focus on how upsetting it is to you, as you love each of them very much, and do not allow any personal accusations. Your aim is not to provide counseling but to offer your perspective that getting together is not as enjoyable as you would like family time to be.

Some families have set general ground rules. If there seems to be a certain subject that is sensitive, suggest that it not be brought up when you are together.

If they refuse to admit there is a problem or cannot agree to reach a compromise for the sake of good manners, then begin inviting each couple over separately in rotation. The important point is to keep a relationship with your children, even if it involves compromises.

∾ *The beginning of strife is like letting out water, so abandon the quarrel before it breaks out. (Proverbs 17:14)*
∾ *For I have been informed concerning you, my brethren . . . that there are quarrels among you. (1 Corinthians 1:11)*

~

15. There is always a fight when my husband's family gets together. I've decided not to attend any more family gatherings. However, my husband does not appreciate my decision. What compromise can we reach?

You married his family when you married him. Therefore, some visiting is worth the effort and the relationship. We

71

are commanded in 1 Peter (3:8) to be harmonious, sympathetic, and kindhearted. Families have very diverse ways of communicating. What you call fighting may just be a healthy discussion to them. Therefore it may be a matter of you needing to extend grace to people who do not do things the way you do.

If your husband understands how uncomfortable it makes you, he may be willing to explain your feelings to the family and ask if guidelines could be set for family gatherings. There are social rules that have prevailed for years, such as "never discuss politics or religion." Maybe there are certain subjects that need to be off-limits at family gatherings.

Finally, if nothing changes, work out a compromise with your spouse on how many gatherings you need to attend and how long you need to stay. Do not be a martyr. Someone in the family will be available to visit with while a ruckus is ongoing. Make it a practice to take handiwork to concentrate on or play with the children.

ꝏ *Keeping away from strife is an honor for a man, but any fool will quarrel. (Proverbs 20:3)*
ꝏ *What is the source of quarrels and conflicts among you? Is not the source your pleasures that wage war in your members? (James 4:1)*

16. **We've been married three years and each holiday has been spent with one of our parents. We want to do something different. How can we handle this?**

How about saying, "Herkimer and I have decided to begin our own family celebrations. We plan to spend this year's holidays alone"? If you have children I certainly encourage this, because your family unit needs to establish your own unique customs apart from the ones each extended family observes.

After you have had a break, decide together how you intend to handle future holidays. Maybe you can spend Thanksgiving with your parents and Christmas with his parents one year, and switch holidays the next. The bottom line is that you are responsible for doing what is best for your family. Set your own schedule and do not be manipulated.

I understand that having family in close proximity is a twofold blessing during the holidays, but with planning and forethought, the delicate balance of building your family and keeping bonds with your extended family can be achieved.

❧ *These are the things which you should do: speak the truth to one another. (Zechariah 8:16)*
❧ *For this reason a man shall leave his father and mother and be joined to his wife, and the two shall become one flesh. (Matthew 19:5)*

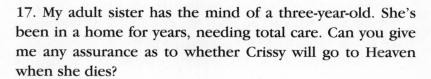

17. My adult sister has the mind of a three-year-old. She's been in a home for years, needing total care. Can you give me any assurance as to whether Crissy will go to Heaven when she dies?

*Y*es, your sister will go to Heaven. When we study the attributes of God, we see that He is a just God. He understands our frailties even more than we do ourselves. We are accountable for the truth we know and if Crissy's intellect is that of a three-year-old, she has not reached an age of being accountable for her spiritual life. Just think, when you recognize her in Heaven, she will be perfect and complete. That will bring you great joy.

∾ *Then the eyes of the blind will be opened and the ears of the deaf will be unstopped. Then the lame will leap like a deer, and the tongue of the mute will shout for joy. For waters will break forth in the wilderness and streams in the Arabah. (Isaiah 35:5, 6)*

∾ *He [God] will wipe away every tear from their eyes. There will be no more death or mourning or crying or pain, for the old order of things has passed away. (Revelation 21:4 NIV)*

~

18. Our elderly mother recently made her burial wishes known. She wants to be cremated. The whole family is up-in-arms about this. Can you tell me if it is okay for Christians to do this?

Cremation has traditionally been avoided by Christians, but there is not any prohibition of it in the Bible. In some countries cremation is the only option the law allows, owing to either health practices, shortage of land, or both.

One reason we prefer burial may be that is the way Christ's body was handled after he died. Other writers in the Bible allude to burial, but the passages probably do not mean to be literal directions. Interestingly, sometimes Christians refuse to accept cremation because they know that on the Resurrection Day the dead in Christ will rise from their graves. However, God can certainly gather our bodies even from ashes and reassemble them in an instant to allow us to be raised with Christ.

Unfortunately, it is likely that none of these comments will have any effect on your family's feelings and may continue to be a point of contention. I understand that this is an emotional and sensitive subject. However, if the family can understand that they are not the ones making this decision but simply honoring your mother's decision, they might be more willing to acquiesce to her wishes. Do your best to keep the topic from fragmenting the family, as once your mother passes on, the members of your family will need one another's support. Concentrate on your mother's wishes, not your own opinions.

Precious in the sight of the LORD is the death of His godly ones. (Psalms 116:15)

For the Lord Himself will descend from heaven with a shout, with the voice of the archangel and with the trumpet of God, and the dead in Christ will rise first. (1 Thessalonians 4:16)

~

19. I believe my cousin, who lost her eighteen-year-old daughter two years ago, is not getting over her daughter's death. What is the length of time for us to grieve healthfully?

Each person grieves at a different rate. You cannot make her move forward in her process, so advice will not help. What you can do is concentrate on being a friend. Contact her often—chat on the phone, drop her a note in the mail, invite her shopping and out to lunch. Allow her to share her feelings at her pace. Remain supportive, but do not pry. One reason people who are grieving separate themselves from others is that we too often try to "fix" them. When you are drowning emotionally, glib solutions, even if they are true, create more anger than answer any of your questions. Through it all, pray continually that she will allow the Holy Spirit to heal her.

For some additional information (found at *www.york-united-kingdom.co.uk/funerals/grief)*, there are five stages of grief that everyone goes through. They are: denial, anger, bargaining, depression, and acceptance.

ᴥ *My soul weeps because of grief; strengthen me according to
Your word. (Psalms 119:28)*
ᴥ *Therefore you too have grief now; but I will see you again,
and your heart will rejoice, and no one will take your joy
away from you. (John 16:22)*

~

**20. My sister's husband has been married before and
shares custody of his two school-age daughters with his
first wife. He insists that because the girls are his blood relatives, they should be his first priority. As you can imagine,
this creates a great deal of stress in my sister's marriage
because all the girls need to do is say, "Daddy, will you . . ."
and he drops everything to go with them. Can you offer my
sister any advice?**

Your sister can choose a nonstressful time to discuss with
him the effect his choices are having on their marriage
and the emotional maturing of his daughters. It is certainly
admirable that he understands his responsibility to them.
However, everyone needs boundaries. It appears the daughters know the emotional power they wield. However, being
able to command Dad's instant response is not good life
training for them. The Bible clearly states that a man's first
obligation after serving God is to cleave (or cling) to his wife.
If we are joined together in unity, no one can come between
us. Since his daughters are able to come between them, he is
not being unified with his wife. He needs to understand that
parents who stand together as one, indivisible before the children, provide security to their children. Because of the
divorce, security is what his daughters are seeking by calling
upon him. It is proper for them to reach out to him for help,
but it is not right for him not to set boundaries on how and

when the help will be supplied. He (probably in ignorance) is contributing to their insecurity by not setting parameters.

∾ *For this reason a man shall leave his father and his mother and be joined to his wife; and they shall become one flesh. (Genesis 2:24)*
∾ *Honor your father and mother (which is the First Commandment with a promise), so that it may be well with you, and that you may live long on the earth. (Ephesians 6:3)*

∾

21. I am almost ten years older than my younger sister. I am out of college while she is still in high school. Recently she discovered that our mother has been reading her diary and other personal correspondence. She is extremely angry. When I asked Mom why she would invade her privacy, Mom said she was only making sure that Sis wasn't into drugs. Do you believe it is ever okay to snoop on your kids in this manner?

The Bible instructs us to seek truth and wisdom. Therefore, contrary to a more popular opinion, I do believe that at times, parents are right to "snoop" on their children. Whether I would agree with your mother in this instance would depend on what your sister's history has been. If she has always been well behaved, brought home the best grades she was capable of receiving, and just generally behaved as a first-rate kid, then I would say that your mom should not have invaded her privacy in the manner you described.

If, on the other hand, your sister has had a history of rebellion, breaking rules, or toying with illegal behavior, then I would say that everything is open to suspicion and subject to search. Even if she is not openly rebellious but is secretive about her activities and evasive regarding who her friends are and where she's been, I would again say that further scrutiny is warranted.

Regarding your sister's anger, just because she does not want to deal with consequences does not mean that consequences do not occur. We do reap what we sow, and if she has behaved in a manner that makes her truthfulness questionable, then your parents had a responsibility to get to the bottom of the cause of her misbehavior.

∽ *There is no secret that is a match for you. (Ezekiel 28:3)*
∽ *Whatever a man sows, this he will also reap. (Galatians 6:7)*

22. This is a second marriage for both my husband and me. We are attempting to build a blended family with my two children and his daughter, all elementary-school-age. Can you give me any advice?

I would be very open in communicating that making your family work is everyone's responsibility. You should pick one night a week to have a family meeting, in which you can teach on the importance of family, what a family is, and what can tear apart a family. Make it clear that Satan's aim is to kill, steal, and destroy (John 10:10), and therefore, as a family, you do not intend to allow him to do any harm within yours. You need to set ground rules for everyone. They should include issues such as privacy, discipline, fighting, and chores. Use the family meetings to discuss problem areas that have come up and to plan future family outings.

I understand that making a blended family work is probably one of the hardest jobs anyone attempts. I would encourage you to hand out a lot of grace—to yourself, your spouse, your children, and his children. Pray for wisdom and direction. Select an activity for the whole family to participate in and incorporate it regularly in your family's schedule. Choose one that everyone can participate in and enjoys. Whether it is movie night, camping, or baseball, the hours you spend involved in it will serve to strengthen your relationships and create a sense of family. If watching movies is enjoyable for the whole family, log on to *www.familytv.org* for a source of family-friendly films.

Finally, you will all need to cut each other a little slack. In the beginning, you will experience a period of adjustment and it will be stressful. However, if you continue to emphasize the family goals and establish a routine in which each member can participate, the adjustments and acceptance of each other will come. (Check out the bibliography for more resources for blended families.)

∾ *The wise woman builds her house, but the foolish tears it down with her own hands. (Proverbs 14:1)*
∾ *To sum up, let all of you be harmonious, sympathetic, brotherly, kindhearted, and humble in spirit; not returning evil for evil, or insult for insult, but giving a blessing instead; for you were called for the very purpose that you might inherit a blessing. (1 Peter 3:8–9)*

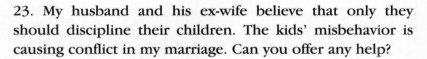

23. My husband and his ex-wife believe that only they should discipline their children. The kids' misbehavior is causing conflict in my marriage. Can you offer any help?

You are faced with a perplexing situation, but before I can give direction, there are some unanswered questions: Are you left to care for them alone or do they only visit when their father is present? Is it possible that when your husband and his ex-wife state they do not want you to discipline that they are really meaning no corporal punishment?

If the children are present only when their father is at home and are still disruptive, the problem may be that their father needs to take the initiative to discipline them so you won't feel the need. However, if your husband and his ex-wife can understand that discipline does not only mean corporal punishment, then you should be allowed to maintain it through structure and order in your home, with clearly set guidelines for expected behavior. Discipline really means "training," and punishment can take many effective forms without ever being physical. It can mean time-out, grounding, extra chores, or removal of privileges.

There appear to be several issues that you have not settled, and you may be wise to ask for a mediator to meet with you, your husband, and his ex-wife. Someone neutral, such as a Christian counselor, can help the three of you set guidelines you all feel comfortable following.

It is vital that the adults reach a compromise so that the children are not the losers, as they surely are right now.

∾ *A child who gets his own way brings shame to his mother.* *(Proverbs 29:15)*
∾ *But if you are without discipline, of which all have become partakers, then you are illegitimate children and not sons.* *(Hebrews 12:8)*

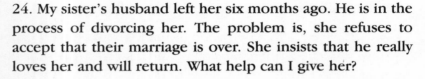

24. My sister's husband left her six months ago. He is in the process of divorcing her. The problem is, she refuses to accept that their marriage is over. She insists that he really loves her and will return. What help can I give her?

You can offer support, kindness, and a listening ear. At the moment she is in the midst of grieving for her lost dreams. It is hard to accept that something is over, especially when we still desperately love the one who has left. One of the ways we keep from facing a failed marriage is to believe that he will return "as soon as he gets it out of his system."

If you remain nonjudgmental, and offer support to her, then at some point you can gently remind her that no one can make a decision for another. God gave a free will to every person. No matter how much she may love him, no matter how much she desires for the marriage to continue, she cannot make her husband love her or remain married to her.

Your best help will be praying for her every day and providing emotional support as she painfully faces reality.

~ *I call Heaven and earth to witness against you today, that I have set before you life and death, the blessing and the curse. So choose life in order that you may live. (Deuteronomy 30:19)*
~ *Yet if the unbelieving one leaves, let him leave. (1 Corinthians 7:15)*

~

25. My brother just announced that he is gay. He was raised in the same Christian home I was. How can he reconcile this reasoning, and am I wrong in believing it is sin?

I will not insult your intelligence or anyone's by insisting that there is a simple explanation for why someone becomes gay.

That being said, your brother was raised in the same household as you and therefore he knows what the Bible says about his choice. You do not need to enlighten him. We are not called to convince him of error; that is the job of the Holy Spirit in each of our lives. What you need to do is to keep the door of communication and acceptance open to him. Jesus said that others will know we are Christians by our love, so concentrate on building your relationship with him. You may need to take the initiative, because he may assume

81

you do not want to have anything to do with him and become withdrawn from your family.

❧ *I will sing of the LORD's great love forever; with my mouth I will make your faithfulness known through all generations. (Psalms 89:1 NIV)*
❧ *This is My commandment, that you love one another, just as I have loved you. (John 15:12)*

~

26. Friends of mine do not use any birth control, believing God will give them the number of children they should have. I do not wish to violate God's laws. What does the Bible say about birth control?

The Bible emphasizes the blessing that children are to us, but it does not directly discuss the issue of birth control. However, God expects us to use wisdom regarding the responsibilities we undertake. Children require a sizable investment from us in terms of time, money, and nurturing. We therefore should plan to bring into the world the number of children for which we are able emotionally and financially to provide care. Psalms (127:5) says, "Happy is the man whose quiver is full." We can only speculate as to whether the Scripture is indicating an actual number or, more probably, if it simply means that the man whose home is blessed by children is happy. I do believe that the Scriptures are clear in expressing that children are a blessing and a joy to a marriage.

❧ *Behold, children are a gift of the LORD, The fruit of the womb is a reward. (Psalms 127:3)*
❧ *But if any of you lacks wisdom, let him ask of God, who gives to all generously and without reproach, and it will be given to him. (James 1:5)*

MARRIAGE

1. I would really like to quit work to stay home and care for our two preschoolers, but my husband does not make enough to support our family. I believe that the Bible teaches that supporting the family is really his responsibility, so I am considering quitting and telling him I've been laid off.

You say it is his responsibility to follow God's command to support the family, but it is okay for you to disregard God's commandment about lying and deceive your husband. I cannot imagine the incalculable damage that will be done to your relationship when he finds out your deception—and he will (if not immediately, certainly when the unemployment checks do not materialize). Also, have you thought about what you are going to say to your conscience? It certainly is not going to keep quiet about your duplicity. Forget it, the deception is not worth it.

Second, while the Bible does teach that the husband is the head of the home, you may be assuming too much by interpreting it to mean sole provider. In today's economy, it often takes both parents' incomes to provide adequately for their family.

Even so, your desire to stay at home and care for your children is not wrong. Make it a matter of prayer. Ask for God to bless your husband's work and open a door for a job that will support your family without having to depend on your income. Discuss with your husband your desire to stay home. Together, plan a course of action that will allow you to work toward this goal. Be open to employment possibilities that will allow you to remain at home, such as beginning a day care in your home, job sharing, or contracting to do office work on behalf of a company from your home.

❧ *Bless our God, O peoples, and sound His praise abroad, who keeps us in life and does not allow our feet to slip. (Psalms 66:8–9)*

∾ *Do not be deceived, God is not mocked; for whatever a man sows, this he will also reap. (Galatians 6:7)*

~

2. I've just discovered that my husband is addicted to cyberporn. I am devastated and determined to divorce him. Our pastor says that would be wrong because God hates divorce. Can that be right?

*M*y heart goes out to you for the pain you are feeling. While you may eventually have to make a decision to divorce, it should not be your first choice. There are several biblical steps that you need to implement first. You need to insist that the two of you go for Christian marriage counseling. A counselor will help you sort through several important aspects of your relationship, such as whether your husband is repentant for his sin and does he wish to mend your marriage.

Since grief and anger are blocking reasonable thinking at this time, I encourage you not to make a life-changing decision right now. Contrary to popular belief, divorce is not a good solution for a bad marriage. If you divorce without addressing the issues you are facing, you almost inevitably will carry them with you into your next marriage. Unsurprisingly, there you will re-encounter the problems. Studies such as one from the Marriage Maintenance Ministry Web site (*www.marriagemaintenance.org*) report that second marriages have a 60 percent chance of facing a second divorce within five years.

He needs to accept that looking at pornography is a sin. While popular philosophy asserts that thinking something is not the same as doing it, Jesus asserted, "If a man looks on a woman in lust, he has committed adultery." (Matthew 5:28

KJV) In the manner of King David, who when confronted with his sin of adultery cried, "Before you, God, and you only have I sinned," your husband needs to accept that his greatest sin is against God and ask for His forgiveness. God's supernatural power can effectively break the hold of addiction. Addictions are terrifying to deal with, but honesty is the first step to overcoming them.

God certainly hates divorce (Malachi 2:16), but He does make provision for it in cases of infidelity, as mentioned in Matthew (5:32). I understand your view of vicarious sex in cyberspace being infidelity. However, in your pain you are stretching the scriptural intention for divorce. I encourage you to seek reconciliation with your husband and with God's help create a better relationship that will testify of God's grace.

Finally, the most important area necessary for your healing will be to forgive your husband. Sometimes we think that *this sin* doesn't deserve to be forgiven. Yet, God always forgives a repentant heart. Do not be hasty in making a decision that you may live to regret. The bibliography can also suggest additional resources.

I suggest you also fast and pray for your marriage. When doing this, ask God to bring peace to each of your minds and hearts so that you can listen to what He is saying.

~ *His own iniquities will capture the wicked, and he will be held with the cords of his sin. (Proverbs 5:22)*
~ *Bearing with one another, and forgiving each other, whoever has a complaint against anyone; just as the Lord forgave you, so also should you. (Colossians 3:13)*

~

3. My husband hates his job. I am fearful that he may decide just to quit without having another one to go to.

Will my compassion for his unhappiness seem like a "go ahead" to quit?

*E*mpathy is a very healing response to a hard situation. From experience, I know how hard it is on the whole family when hubby works a job he does not like. However, consider what purpose God may have for him at this time. Has he sought God's will for his life? Is he actively seeking other employment? Each day, pray that God will give him grace to face his work. Pray for a new opportunity to open up in God's time. Also, pray for spiritual growth in your spouse that he will seek the best for the family. Allow God time to work. Keep an open ear when your husband grouses, allowing him the freedom to vent. Do not try to solve the problem. Sometimes just verbalizing our frustration allows us to see the solution. Pray that this will be so for your spouse.

∾ *Six days you shall labor and do all your work. (Exodus 20:9)*
∾ *Rejoice with those who rejoice, and weep with those who weep. (Romans 12:15)*

4. **Now that we have the two children we both wanted, I do not want to have sex anymore. My husband says that the Bible teaches that I have to have sex whenever he wants it. It does not really say that, does it?**

*Y*es, it does say that we're not to withhold sex from our spouses (1 Corinthians 7:2–5). However, that is the *letter* of the law, not the intent. God is merely affirming that good sex contributes to a good marriage. A good physical relationship is one way of avoiding infidelities. It is the "why go out for a hamburger when you can get steak at home" school of thought. I would discuss with your husband why you do not enjoy sex. Share with him what would help you enjoy it more. Dr. DiLeo, an ob/gyn practitioner and author of *The Anxious Parents Guide to Pregnancy*, states that a young mother's lack of sex drive usually stems from exhaustion. Maybe your husband needs to assume responsibility for bathing the children and putting them to bed several nights a week in order to give you some rest.

God gave sex as a gift to the marriage relationship. Picture yourself holding out a beautifully wrapped present to your friend in which you have wrapped the most perfect gift you could find. You are fairly popping at the seams with excitement over this fantastic, wonderful thing that you want her to find inside. That really is an apt picture of God's intention when He gave us a sexual relationship. Your reticence regarding sex may stem from childhood teaching. It may also be an outgrowth of sexual permissiveness before marriage, which can lead to negative sexual feelings. One such study is available on *www.personal.umich.edu*, by William R. Mattox Jr. I would encourage you to pray for God to give you a different perspective on sex. Ask Him to help you enjoy its contribution to the good of your marriage.

However, your husband needs to also re-examine his attitude toward what he feels is your *obligation* to have sex whenever he wishes. Sex is not about control. In other words, we do not engage in sex with our spouses because we *have to*. I do not imagine there are any of us who have not said, "Not tonight, honey." Nor can I imagine anything less exciting than "duty sex." I would encourage you and your husband each to explore your attitudes about the marriage relationship with a competent Christian counselor.

A good book to read regarding the joy of the sexual relationship in marriage is *Sex Begins in the Kitchen,* by Dr. Kevin Leman.

∾ *May he kiss me with the kisses of his mouth! For your love is better than wine. (Song of Solomon 1:2)*
∾ *The wife does not have authority over her own body, but the husband does; and likewise also the husband does not have authority over his own body, but the wife does. (1 Corinthians 7:4)*

∾

5. My husband and I were unbelievers when we married. Since then I have become a believer and am wondering if God makes a provision for getting a divorce from an unbeliever. I know it is not good for our home to be unequally yoked together.

No, God does not make a provision for getting a divorce from an unbelieving spouse. In fact, just the opposite is expressed in the Bible. In 1 Corinthians (7:12), He tells us that if an unbelieving spouse is willing to remain with us, we should allow it. By our actions and attitudes, we can be instrumental in leading them into a relationship with Jesus Christ.

As sometimes happens, when spouses have two opposite viewpoints as you may be experiencing, it can lead to the temptation to believe you would be better off without him. I encourage you to instead see it as a wonderful opportunity to minister to your husband in a godly manner and (I hope) win him to Christ.

∾ *"For I hate divorce," says the LORD, the God of Israel. (Malachi 2:16)*
∾ *And a woman who has an unbelieving husband and he consents to live with her, she must not send her husband away. (1 Corinthians 7:13)*

6. I love to entertain guests, but my husband and kids absolutely hate having people over. How can we reach a compromise?

*B*eing hospitable is stressed in Scripture. I commend you for wishing to exercise this gift. It is true that many men prefer their home to be reserved exclusively for their families. Perhaps your husband works a high-stress job and wishes home to be a haven for him. You need to take into account your husband's and children's personalities when looking for a reason for their reticence.

It may help if you approach him quietly and explain how important it is for you to be hospitable. Show how its importance is stressed in Scripture. Ask if you could, together, set parameters by which the whole family can live with regarding entertaining others. Maybe if they know you will be having company the third Thursday of each month, for instance, it will become an accepted part of your family's routine. Who knows, after a time they may even look forward to it.

But I am also wondering if your family's dread stems more from what happens *before* you have guests over than actually having guests in your home. I grew up in a family of five kids. More often than not we had other people eating at our table or sleeping in our beds some time every week. We loved it. My mom knew the secret of effortless hospitality. The best motive for inviting people into your home isn't for the purpose of demonstrating what a great cook you are or how lovely your home is but to share your life. If you feel that everything must be perfect before someone can come over, I imagine everyone in the family gets stressed preparing for company. You may need to examine what your incentive is to entertain. Do you do it because you love the company of people? Can you sit and visit without stressing if there are toys on the floor or dirty dishes in the sink? Do you spend your company time jumping up to wash dishes or put together last-minute appetizers? If so, you may inadvertently be making them feel they are an inconvenience. It does not matter if you dine on fine china or paper plates, what matters is the fellowship. (See the bibliography for some resources on entertaining.)

∾ *He who is generous will be blessed, for he gives some of his food to the poor. (Proverbs 22:9)*
∾ *Be hospitable to one another without complaint. (1 Peter 4:9)*

⌒

7. Why would someone remain in an unhappy marriage?

There are undoubtedly a myriad of reasons people remain married, but one important one for Christians to remember is that there are no scriptural grounds for divorce because of unhappiness. It is interesting that some people never understand that being happy is a choice they can make. It is not a spouse's (or anyone's) responsibility to make someone else happy. Everyone who has been married any length of time can remember periods when they have been unhappy in their marriage. It is a fact of life that there are hard times in any long-term relationship, but to leave it because you are unhappy is unwise.

In fact, John W. Kennedy, in "Special Report: Divorce Has Become Big Business in America" (*Pentecostal Evangel,* 28 July 2002, p. 15), reports that rarely are problems in a marriage solved by divorce. He explains that because each partner contributes to the problems, when the marriage is dissolved, each walks away with painful baggage that is included in the new relationship if they remarry.

A recent study by the Coalition for Marriage, Families and Couples Education shows that people who went through hard times in their marriage, but who remained together, discovered that within five years the problems that had caused them grief had been resolved. It further found that the partners said they were very glad they had stayed in their relationship.

Another correlating study of 645 unhappy households found that within five years of confessing that they were unhappy in their marriage, 80 percent of the couples were happy. In other words, problems pass if you work on them.

Do you still have room for more research? One other study reported in the *Idaho Statesman* (13 July 2002), entitled "Maybe I Do" featured fifty-five couples who had moved from unhappy to happy marriages found that the improvements in the marriages happened in one of three ways: by waiting it out (time does heal; situations do improve); by deliberately working on the problems to solve them; or by finding alternate ways to improve their own happiness and build a good life despite a less-than-happy marital relationship. For more information on the study, you can log onto the Web site, *www.smartmarriages.com.*

∽ *It's better not to make a promise at all than to make one and not keep. (Ecclesiastes 5:5 CEV)*
∽ *So they are no longer two, but one flesh. What therefore God has joined together, let no man separate. (Matthew 19:6)*

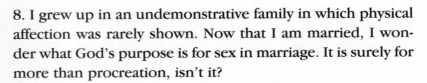

8. I grew up in an undemonstrative family in which physical affection was rarely shown. Now that I am married, I wonder what God's purpose is for sex in marriage. It is surely for more than procreation, isn't it?

*Y*es, God's purpose for the sexual relationship in marriage is much more than to populate the earth. God sees sex as a gift to marriage. In this gift He has included a wonderful *glue* that binds a husband and wife together physically and spiritually in a way nothing else can. Sex is not just an act. It is a bond. At times you and your husband will hit rough spots in your marriage, in which communication will be hard. If you will continue to reach out to each other sexually, you will find that it will help carry you through times of stress.

There is an assumption in the world that all Christians are frigid prudes while those who are not religious are vibrant sexual beings. Not true. During the '70s, *Redbook* magazine did a survey of 100,000 women and made some very interesting discoveries. One of their findings was that married Christian women reported having more satisfying relationships and enjoyable sex lives than any other category of women.

I didn't then, nor do I now, find that surprising. A key ingredient in a woman's sexual and relational satisfaction is feeling secure. Christian women today still, by far, expect that when they marry they and their spouse will remain married until one or the other dies. That contributes to a sense of contentment, which frees them to relax and enjoy themselves.

Each time you and your husband commit your love to each other in your physical relationship, breathe a little prayer that God will use it to bind you to each other emotionally.

∾ *As a loving hind and a graceful doe, let her breasts satisfy you at all times; be exhilarated always with her love. (Proverbs 5:19)*
∾ *Marriage is to be held in honor among all, and the marriage bed is to be undefiled. (Hebrews 13:4)*

∼

9. I oppose interracial marriages. Doesn't the Bible support my viewpoint?

God does not oppose interracial marriage. It may be that you are thinking of the admonitions in the Old Testament to the Jewish nation in which God instructed them not to let their children intermarry with the children of the nations around them. If you look at those passages, you will see that the reason God did not allow intermarriage was that He knew that the spouses from ungodly nations would teach their pagan ways to the Israelites and lead them astray.

Your *personal* belief may be that interracial marriages are unwise because of social acceptability, but I would urge you to be honest with your children and stress that this is your opinion, not a biblical teaching.

God still opposes intermarriage between believers and unbelievers. The nations through which the Children of Israel passed en route to the Promised Land were nations of extremely pagan beliefs; they practiced human sacrifice, ritualistic prostitution, and many other abominations. God knew that when people of belief intermarry with unbelievers, there is a strong possibility that the believers will adopt the heathen practices. As a side note, whenever a believer disobeys God and marries an unbeliever, God validates their free choice and comes alongside to support the union. Not because He approves of it, but because He so definitely disapproves of divorce.

∾ *From the nations concerning which the Lord had said to the sons of Israel, "You shall not associate with them, nor shall they associate with you, for they will surely turn your heart away after their gods." (1 Kings 11:2)*
∾ *For He Himself is our peace, who made both groups into one and broke down the barrier of the dividing wall. (Ephesians 2:14)*

10. I am in the middle of my midlife change and I can tell my emotions are not stable. In fact, I am wondering if my husband is going to stay with me. Shouldn't God have planned this better?

*Y*ou can add this question to your growing list of "What I Am Going to Ask God When I Get to Heaven." You know that all through life women get to enjoy only one week out of each month. First, we have PMS and the next week our period. The third week is filled with apologizing to everyone for the things we did and said in the previous two weeks! It is no wonder we question His planning!

I, too, am experiencing the *joys* of change and am amazed at my emotional instability. As a matter of fact it reminds me of adolescent angst on steroids. I will admit that I have, on more than one occasion, gone to bed at 6 P.M. because I simply was not able to control my mouth. I knew if I wanted my family to continue to love their mother and wife, I'd better remove myself, temporarily, from their midst. I now fully understand cultures that build "that time of the month" huts at the back of their property for the women to dwell in. I'd love to have a place like that.

Seek out a doctor and tell her all of your symptoms. If you are brave, ask your family to write down what they see has changed in your behavior and take it along for discussion (or evidence that you need help). Be willing to take her advice. Be open with your family and discuss the changes and ask for their grace and forgiveness. Above all, remember that God can see us through all stages of life.

Bear in mind that the beauty of the Christian life is that we do not have to place our reliance upon ourselves. We can ask for and obtain grace and help from God. The Holy Spirit is called our Helper, and He can help us survive these emotional years with grace.

❧ *I said, "I will guard my ways that I may not sin with my*

*tongue; I will guard my mouth as with a muzzle."
(Psalms 39:1)*
∾ *We confidently say, "the Lord is my helper, I will not be
afraid. What will man do to me?" (Hebrews 13:6)*

∾

**11. I can trace the problems in our marriage directly back to
my husband's immaturity and selfishness. For instance, if I
hadn't allowed him to make all the financial decisions, we
would not be facing financial ruin. I think many times
women are better leaders than men. Surely male leadership
is not all that important today, is it?**

What makes God's Word so dependable is its unchange-
ableness. Yes, male leadership is extremely important
within a marriage. It is the role God has appointed to the
man. However, leadership should not mean dictatorship.
Each partner brings to the marriage different skills. Maybe
you are a better financial manager and the handling of your
finances needs to be under your direction. These types of
practical issues need to be discussed and divided between
the partners according to individual gifts.

However, there is another aspect you might also consider.
You may have unwittingly contributed to your spouse's inef-
fective leadership by your attitude toward him. At the moment
you seem to have trouble remembering any redeeming qualities in your spouse. One of a man's greatest needs is to feel
adequate about himself. None of us exist in a vacuum, and
degrading remarks can contribute to negative behavior. People
are self-fulfilling prophecies. If you speak about them as if they
already exhibit the qualities you desire, they will often appear.

You might ask yourself what kind of a man your father was.
If your father exhibited the negative characteristics you see in

your husband, you are possibly heaping your anger toward Dad onto your spouse and refusing to extend grace to him.

Finally, allowing your husband to lead does not mean you should sit idly by while he makes disastrous decisions. God calls us to be helpers to our husbands, not doormats. You have a very important role: that of influence. I am not talking *nagging*, but you have the power and responsibility to give appropriate advice and counsel. Each person left to make decisions alone has blind spots. Your husband needs your perspective on issues in order to see the whole picture. Pray about the right time to offer counsel. Examine your attitude, for if you give your counsel in a derogatory manner, your husband may become defensive and not be willing to hear the information you have to present. Choose a time where there are few distractions and approach the subject nonjudgmentally. If the problem is great and has been ongoing for several years, it will take time to learn good communication techniques, but there are books available (see the bibliography) and Christian counselors who can offer guidance.

❧ *Then the Lord God said, "It is not good for the man to be alone. I will make a helper suitable for him." (Genesis 2:18)*
❧ *For the husband is the head of the wife as Christ also is the head of the church, He Himself being the Savior of the body. But as the church is subject to Christ, so also the wives ought to be to their husbands in everything. Husbands, love your wives, just as Christ also loved the church and gave Himself up for her. (Ephesians 5:23–25)*

⁓

12. We are newly married and my husband has two more years before he graduates from college. I discovered last month that I am pregnant and my husband is furious. He

has suggested that it would be best if I got an abortion. I do not want one, but I do not want to bring an unwanted child into the world either. What should I do?

*T*here's an old Jewish proverb that says if you want to give God a good laugh, tell him your plans. While starting your family was not in your five-year plan, it has happened. Accepting that life does not turn out as we envisioned is a mark of maturity. Many times detours become our greatest blessings. The new life growing within you is precious, and I encourage you to rejoice in this gift. A baby requires adjustments even when its birth is planned.

God assures us that He will bring good out of any situation if we trust His care, and you are not factoring in what unexpected bonus may come from having this child at this time in your lives. My cousin and his wife struggled to find a solution that would allow him to finish his degree, Mom to support the family, and still provide care for their preschooler. They solved it by Dale's accepting responsibility for four-year-old Kerri's care while Mom worked full-time. Each day, dad with his briefcase, and Kerri, toting her Strawberry Shortcake lunchbox, were a familiar sight on the campus of Northwest Nazarene University. Kerri sat quietly in class playing with her toys while Dad completed his studies Today, Kerri, a young mother herself, still has a special bond with her dad forged during her early days spent solely with Daddy going to "big people's" school.

While having an abortion is a legal option, it would be unkind of me to not warn you of the possibility of Post-Abortion Syndrome. PAS is a form of post-traumatic stress syndrome, such as experienced by veterans after the Vietnam War. Although the symptoms vary and sometimes do not surface until years after the event, they are nonetheless real and should be dealt with. For more information you may log on to *www.safehavenministries.com*. Sometimes the method of cure you seek will have repercussions far greater than the problem you are seeking to solve.

Together, evaluate what having a child will require from both of you. Maybe it means your husband will graduate in three years instead of two. It may mean he will cram for finals while walking the floor with a crying baby, but it can be done. Many have done it before you. We serve a creative God, who has passed on this creativity to His children. If you brainstorm, you will be amazed at the myriad of workable options you can find for balancing school and this new life. Be honest about your disappointment and frustration, but then put it aside and rejoice in the upcoming event.

∽ *Your eyes have seen my unformed substance; and in Your book were all written the days that were ordained for me, when as yet there was not one of them. (Psalms 139:16)*
∽ *Some of you say, "We can do anything we want to." But I tell you that not everything is good for us. (1 Corinthians 6:12 CEV)*

∽

13. Does God have just one special person for us to marry?

I do not believe that God has prechosen our mates, but I am certain He is very interested in whom we choose and what criteria we use. He has left us with good tools to help us make wise decisions: the Bible, His Holy Spirit, wisdom, and knowledge. He demonstrates through his Word that He expects us to be wise in our choices, and understand that what we do affects who we become.

The danger in believing that God has prechosen our mate is that it tends to make us apathetic in how we evaluate those we date. The most important aspect of choosing our mate is to desire the traits that God commends in a person. Scripture emphasizes character and spiritual attributes as laudable qualities in a person with whom we align our life. Focus on your relationship with God, concentrating on learning to discern His voice in order to feel confident on hearing His guidance for every aspect of your life, including marriage.

Just one more word of advice: Should you discern that you did not listen to God when you chose your mate and now are contemplating divorcing him/her in order to find the right person, do not proceed any further. Once you make a choice and marry, God honors your decision. That mate is now the right one for you until death separates you. Your responsibility becomes growing in grace and blessing the one you've committed your life to.

∽ *With Your counsel You will guide me. (Psalms 73:24)*
∽ *Don't copy the behavior and customs of this world, but let God transform you into a new person by changing the way you think. Then you will know what God wants you to do, and you will know how good and pleasing and perfect his will really is. (Romans 12:2 NLT)*

∽

14. My husband has suggested some things we could try to spice up our sex life. How do I determine if they are okay or not?

I am hesitant to give an opinion on someone's sexual practices. I know some people consider that making love with the light on is risqué. Fortunately, we can turn to God's Word and find guidelines for ourselves. The Song of Solomon is a very erotic love story, and by reading it, you can see that God views the sexual relationship as something good.

There are two basic guidelines you and your husband can use to determine how you want to celebrate your love life.

- First of all, do both of you wish to do it? Coercing someone to try something only you want is not good.
- Is it harmful to your body? There are sexual practices that may even be commonly practiced that can or do cause bodily harm and should be avoided.

God did not design marriage so that his gift of sex came hampered with a lot of don'ts. If you and your husband both wish to try something new, do it.

There are good Christian marriage books out on the market. Some will answer your questions more explicitly. Please see the bibliography at the end of the book for a list of them.

෴ *Let your fountain be blessed, and rejoice in the wife of your youth. (Proverbs 5:18)*
෴ *Marriage is to be held in honor among all, and the marriage bed is to be undefiled. (Hebrews 13:4)*

~

15. My husband does not like any of my friends. How should I handle this?

*H*as he ever mentioned why he does not like them? If you ask him to explain why he feels toward them as he does, it may give you insight into your friendships. Maybe it is a personal perspective. He may feel their conversation is uninteresting in the same way we are disinterested when he and his friends discuss who is starting for the Rams on Monday Night Football (and no offense meant to the females who *are* interested in who is starting for the Rams). If the problem seems to be a lack of common ground, make plans to see your friends when he is gone out on his own pursuits, like Monday Night Football. It may work better for you to meet them outside of the hours you and he have together, so meet for lunch.

Sometimes our husband may not like our friends because he thinks we'd rather spend our free time with them than stay at home with him. If this is the problem, examine the amount of time you spend with them in person or on the phone talking to them and adjust it.

Sometimes husbands may not appreciate the influence that our friends have on us. Ask yourself if your friends encourage you to spend money you don't necessarily have or neglect your responsibilities when you are out with them.

If your solution has been to find a couple you both enjoy spending time with, you may discover that proposition to be a difficult one. For some reason, the women we like often marry men who we do not care for, and men often would rather their friend had married a different woman. So do not be discouraged if such a friendship does not materialize.

Finally, sometimes they believe "You have me, why do you need anyone else?" If this is the case, you need to explain how vital girlfriends are to our sanity. Whatever compromise you can work out, go with it, because we need to have girlfriends.

෨ *Two are better than one because they have a good return for their labor. For if either of them falls, the one will lift up his companion. But woe to the one who falls when there is not another to lift him up. (Ecclesiastes 4:9–10)*
෨ *Then he gave orders to the centurion for him to be kept in custody and yet have some freedom, and not to prevent any of his friends from ministering to him. (Acts 24:23)*

～

16. My husband and I have been married for just over a year and last week had our first fight. I was upset by the anger and unkindness we each showed the other. My husband

says it is normal to fight. How can we distinguish between good and bad fighting?

*Y*ou need to set down some ground rules for handling the next one. (Yes, there will be a next one.) One of the best skills we can learn in any relationship, but especially in marriage, is how to fight fairly. Disagreeing with someone, even that man of our dreams, is a normal way of life. If we agreed on everything, then one of us would be superfluous. But if a fight leaves us feeling damaged emotionally, then that is not good. Here are some rules for having a fair fight:

- Stick to the issue at hand—do not bring in secondary issues as ammunition because you are angry, such as, "By the way, I have always hated the way you insist on squeezing the toothpaste tube in the middle."
- Do not dredge up wrongs done before.
- Do keep your tone of voice below forty decibels.
- Do reach a compromise you can both agree on.
- Do set a time limit on how long you will "discuss" it before you agree to disagree. Do not go to bed angry.

Fighting, like all communication skills, take practice and agreement on rules. If you make it your goal to understand each other instead of winning, you'll be more productive also.

By wisdom a house is built, and by understanding it is established. (Proverbs 24:3)
And the peace of God, which surpasses all comprehension, will guard your hearts and your minds in Christ Jesus. (Philippians 4:7)

~

17. My husband and I have reached an impasse in our marriage because of problems with his anger. I am considering

a separation and am wondering if that is the same, in God's eyes, as getting a divorce?

God looks on our hearts. It is your motive for the separation that is important. If you are asking for a separation period so that both of you can work on the problem, I feel you are doing a good thing. For instance, if there has been abuse in your marriage, which may be the case with his anger, it is better to spend some time apart because if you remain a situation may escalate into violence. Second, if one spouse is not committed to the marriage and uses the relationship for convenience, separating will, it is hoped, produce the result of a wake-up call.

The important consideration is to know what your goal is for the relationship. It may involve bringing in a mediator to help you clarify the expectations and resolve the differences.

Most important, keep the whole process bathed in prayer.

∾ *Do not look at his appearance or at the height of his stature, because I have rejected him; for God sees not as man sees, for man looks at the outward appearance, but the LORD looks at the heart. (1 Samuel 16:7)*
∾ *For perhaps he was for this reason separated from you for a while, that you would have him back forever. (Philemon 1:15)*

∼

18. My husband and I married against my parents' objections. Now my husband is acting just like my parents did, trying to order me around, being the boss. We are both Christians, why can't I be treated as an adult?

Reaching the age of twenty-one and being legally free to do what we want and make decisions on our own does not constitute adulthood. Being an adult means accepting responsibility for our actions and attitudes. You admit that you disregarded your parents' authority by marrying against their counsel. They might have seen attributes in both of your lives that made marriage an unwise choice, at least at that time. I am not saying that we must always have our parents' blessing before we make a decision, for sometimes that will be an impossibility; however, you indicate that you disregarded their input when you chose your mate.

God uses authority to develop His character in our lives. Authority is divided into family, government, church, and business. When we step out from under the protection of one authority, God uses another to try to make us face the problem. I am not saying your marriage was a mistake. I am saying that there were negative areas you needed to conquer before you made that choice. You may have seen your marriage as an escape, but God is using it to develop your character.

I cannot judge whether or not your husband is bossing you or simply making a request. However, I know God is willing to produce good in our lives from every situation if we allow Him to. Pray for a gentle and contrite spirit. Ask God for wisdom. Learn to communicate with your husband and listen to what he is saying. For in truth, God is also using you to develop godliness in your husband.

∽ *A man who hardens his neck after much reproof will suddenly be broken beyond remedy. (Proverbs 29:1)*
∽ *The wife must see to it that she respects her husband. (Ephesians 5:33)*

∽

19. My husband occasionally swears in front of the kids. He says it is an honest expression of his emotions and I should just expect it.

*I*t probably is an honest expression of his emotions, but it is not a righteous expression, nor a mature one. Nevertheless, if your husband is a believer, his spirit is reminding him that the Third Commandment commands us not to misuse God's name. If you nag him about it, he will (in the way of all of us) simply dig in his heels and refuse to change. When you back off and allow God to speak to him regarding it, he will find Him harder to ignore.

However, if your husband is an unbeliever, simply ignore it, because you are focusing on the wrong thing. He needs to be born again before he can understand the spiritual significance of wrong habits. The Bible tells us that when we marry an unbeliever it is the witness of our life and not our words that will convince them to serve God.

Whether our spouse is a believer or unbeliever, our job is never to be their conscience. However, as a parent, we are responsible to train our children. Therefore, if your children swear, you should refuse to allow it and discipline them when they continue. If they point out that Daddy swears, explain that Daddy is an adult and is allowed privileges that children are not allowed.

∾ *You shall not misuse the name of the LORD your God. (Exodus 20:7 NIV)*
∾ *Don't use foul or abusive language. Let everything you say be good and helpful, so that your words will be an encouragement to those who hear them. (Ephesians 4:29 NLT)*

~

20. My husband wants to spend all his free time with his hunting and fishing buddies, and the kids and I are feeling neglected. Can this be changed?

From my perspective (and I have been married for almost thirty years), the hardest part of a marriage is accepting our spouse and allowing him to be who he is. However, I understand your loneliness and how much your children need a daddy; so, yes, there is something you can do to attempt a change. You need to make an appeal to your husband for some of his time.

Making an appeal is an honorable biblical custom. It is a method God allows us to use to try to persuade someone in authority to change his mind. The Book of Esther is a story that demonstrates the power of a proper appeal. In the book (which is one story), Queen Esther was faced with seeing her people, the Jews, annihilated, unless she could persuade her husband, the king, to countermand his previous order to kill all of them. Obviously, the king was not a godly or good man, but that does not make a difference in whether we can make an appeal or not.

If you read her story, you will see that she did some specific things to make her appeal. In short, they were:

- She prayed about it.
- She chose the time of her appeal carefully.
- She was willing to accept the outcome.

History shows that because she was successful in her appeal and the Jewish people were allowed to defend themselves, the nation of Israel was saved.

In order for it to be a correct appeal and not manipulation, you must have your mind and heart clean before God and, most important, be willing to accept the outcome even if it is not what you had hoped.

Prepare your appeal to your husband by praying about it. Plan what you will say, and offer options for him. For example, if you ask him to pay more attention to you and the children, that request is probably too open-ended. He may not understand what is expected of him. Instead, explain how you are feeling, tell him how much it means to you and the kids to do things with him, and ask him if he could set aside one evening a week or one weekend a month in which to do a family activity.

Even if he initially refuses, accept it calmly and keep praying that God will open his eyes to the responsibility he carries in his family. Prayer can change the most stubborn man.

∾ *And the king said to Esther on the second day also as they drank their wine at the banquet, "What is your petition, Queen Esther? It shall be granted you. And what is your request? Even to half of the kingdom it shall be done." (Esther 7:2)*

∾ *For the appeal we make does not spring from error or impure motives, nor are we trying to trick you. (1 Thessalonians 2:3 NIV)*

~

21. How can my husband and I quit fighting so much about money?

You can quit fighting about money by neutralizing its power. Oftentimes, in a marriage, money is about control—about one person having more power than the other person because they make all the decisions about how it will be spent. This is unhealthy. Money itself is impartial, but the way we use it can produce good or evil. If both spouses remember that everything you possess comes to you out of God's goodness, it will help you not take ownership of it.

The way to be in command of your money is for you and your husband to sit down together and create a budget that covers living expenses and includes plans for future spending. A budget should also include an allowance for each of you—money that is purely yours, to be spent at your discretion, and for which you do not have to give an accounting. If either of you needs something over and above this allowance, both of you need to agree before you can spend it.

 ∾ *He who loves money will not be satisfied with money, nor he who loves abundance with its income. (Ecclesiastes 5:10)*
 ∾ *For the love of money is a root of all sorts of evil. (1 Timothy 6:10)*

∾

22. My husband and I sometimes rent adult movies to watch before we make love. Would you consider that okay?

No. While watching adult movies together is a sexual turn-on, it also opens the door to lust because it brings another person(s), albeit celluloid, into your marriage. God calls lust a sin. It is also a shortcut to developing a rich and satisfying sexual relationship between you and your husband. There are many things you can do to enrich your sexual relationship, but watching sexy movies is not something you wish to invite into your bedroom. Instead, add things that are just between you and him. God is not pleased when we participate in things that are contrary to His word, and by watching adult movies you are contributing to the plague of improper entertainment with which our world is flooded.

There is nothing wrong with trying to be more creative in your sex life. If you need some ideas, you can read *The Gift of Sex: A Christian Guide to Sexual Fulfillment.* (See the bibliography for a listing of this book.)

 ∾ *I have made a covenant with my eyes; How then could I gaze at a virgin? (Job. 31:1)*
 ∾ *If your hand or your foot causes you to stumble, cut it off and throw it from you; it is better for you to enter life crippled*

or lame, than to have two hands or two feet and be cast into the eternal fire. If your eye causes you to stumble, pluck it out and throw it from you. It is better for you to enter life with one eye, than to have two eyes and be cast into the fiery hell. (Matthew 8:8–9)

~

23. My husband refuses to cultivate his boss's favor. It could help him so much professionally if he would only see the wisdom of paying attention to him, inviting him over for meals, and asking his advice. Can you help me convince him?

My advice is probably the same as your husband's. Gaining advancement through favoritism, while a fine old professional custom, is fully against God's teachings. You need to recognize that your husband really works for God. It is His pleasure we need to seek, not that of an earthly boss.

This does not mean that your husband needs to shun any communication with his boss. For whoever is in authority over him is worthy of respect because of his position. As long as your husband does his job to the best of his ability, he can rely on Gods prospering him in His time. God's favor is much more dependable than man's. My advice is for you not to interfere and leave your husband to do his job in his own way. He needs your support, trust, and prayers. Above all, he needs a boost to his ego that your expression of confidence in his capabilities will give.

∾ *Now his master saw that the LORD was with him and how the LORD caused all that he did to prosper in his hand. (Genesis 39:3)*
∾ *My brothers, as believers in our glorious Lord Jesus Christ, don't show favoritism. (James 2:1 NIV)*

24. My husband and I fight constantly about discipline, money, and division of responsibilities. I really feel that the stress in our home because of this fighting is traumatic to our children and we should get a divorce. Am I right?

Fighting is very stressful on everyone in a home, but studies still demonstrate that divorce is a lifelong trauma your children carry with them even into adulthood. Judith Wallerstein, in "Adult Children of Divorce" (*www.blackwomens health.com*), reports that children of divorce are four times more likely to encounter a divorce in their own marriage.

You are also correct in your assessment that your fighting is hard on your children emotionally. You and your husband should get counseling to learn techniques for reaching compromise on issues in which you differ. Not only will it reduce the tension in the home, it will demonstrate to your children that problems can be resolved. You will have taught your children a valuable truth when you demonstrate to them that bad times can be worked through to a good resolution. As a side note, maybe you need to learn that you do not have to put your dog in every fight. William James said, "The art of being wise is the art of knowing what to overlook." Proverbs agrees, for it says, "A fool shows his annoyance at once, but a prudent man overlooks an insult" (12:16 NIV). Some things are worth disagreeing over, but many things are not. A lot of quarreling occurs because we do not learn when to walk away over nonessentials. It is important to remember that a marriage is a melding of two people from different points of view, and just because his opinion does not coincide with yours, it does not make his view any less viable.

I cannot stress too strongly the damage done to children through their parents' divorce. The bottom line is that you do not keep additional options available when you choose one of them. It is impossible to have your cake and eat it too. When you choose to marry, you no longer keep open the option to date, and, in the same way, it is my personal opinion that after having children, your option for divorce needs to be closed. You and your husband can choose to act like adults and provide a safe home for your children. They deserve the security a two-parent family gives.

At no time am I saying an abusive situation needs to be endured, but the vast majority of breakups, if we are honest, do not stem from abuse. John W. Kennedy, in an article in the *Pentecostal Evangel* (28 July 2002), reports that "Studies indicate that 60 percent of divorces result not from domestic violence, psychological abuse or adultery, but from low-level conflicts that are never resolved." I urge you to set aside your differences and work together to create a sanctuary in which your children can be physically and emotionally safe.

❧ *The wise woman builds her house, but the foolish tears it down with her own hands. (Proverbs 14:1)*
❧ *What is the source of quarrels and conflicts among you? Is not the source your pleasures that wage war in you? (James 4:1)*

CHILDREN

1. Many of my friends' adult children are living their lives contrary to the values I know were instilled in them when small. Is there a key I can implement that will ensure I am teaching my children lasting values?

Yes, there are principles you can use, which when aligned with prayer, are a powerful facilitator of change. However, the bottom line is your children are given the same freedom God gives everyone: freedom to choose whom to serve.

The probabilities of them following in our footsteps are greater when we not only teach our values but live them out in our everyday life. I am personally convinced that the greatest factor in whether or not children follow what you have taught them is whether your life demonstrates what you say you believe. Actions speak louder than words.

Finally, let me remind you that God is the perfect parent and his first two children rebelled. Ask God to help you do the very best you can and leave the result in His hands. Even if it appears they do not to value Christianity, the whole story is not done until life is over. There is always room for hope fueled by prayer.

∾ *Only be careful, and watch yourselves closely so that you do not forget the things your eyes have seen or let them slip from your heart as long as you live. (Deuteronomy 4:9 NIV)*
∾ *I have no greater joy than this, to hear of my children walking in the truth. (3 John 4)*

∾

2. I see many adult children returning home. We are thoroughly enjoying our empty nest. Are we wrong not to allow our adult kids to move back home?

I understand the desire you and your husband have to build a second life for just you two, but a family is for life. When you agreed to have children, you agreed to be there for the long haul—including toddlerhood, adolescence, and adulthood. There are requests you can justifiably refuse. For instance, if they ask to return home to avoid paying rent or to be able to afford an exotic vacation or a new sports car, do not hesitate to say no if you wish.

But at times, even adults need a haven, and you should be open to the possibility that your support may be needed even after your children have left home. It is our goal as parents to train our children to accept personal responsibility, but sometimes catastrophic events happen, and, though grown, they may need a sanctuary while they put their life back together. One example for which they may need you is if they go through a devastating divorce in which all personal belongings had to be sold and he/she needs time to regroup emotionally and financially.

If the time comes that an adult child asks to return home, the single most important thing you can do is set boundaries/expectations *before* they move back. The agreement may even be typed up and signed by all of you. It should include, among other considerations: the length of time for the stay, what remuneration you expect, what chores they will be responsible for, and what rules they will abide by. If you are concerned that it may happen to you, a good book to read to help you prepare is *Boundaries,* which is listed in the bibliography.

❧ *Rescue the weak and needy. (Psalms 82:4)*
❧ *So he got up and came to his father. But while he was still a long way off, his father saw him and felt compassion for him, and ran and embraced him and kissed him. (Luke 15:20)*

3. My kids, ages five and seven, do not do their chores correctly, so I always redo them afterward. I believe that gives them an example to go by, but they do not seem to be learning. What else can I do?

The Bible (Proverbs 22:6) indicates that training our children to do right is very important. It is true that you have to demonstrate the correct way to do something, but continually finding fault with their efforts will discourage them from trying.

Let me demonstrate it this way to you. How would you feel if every time you finished folding the laundry your mother came over, took everything out of the closets and drawers, and redid them? Would you feel frustrated? Degraded? Discouraged? There is a very simple rule you need to learn about people: Praise what you want repeated; ignore what you want to go away. Now obviously that will not work in everything, but when it comes to chores, it will work like a charm. When little Suzie makes her bed and the left-hand side of the bedspread is hanging onto the floor, while the right-hand side barely reaches the right edge of the bed, you say, "I love the way you put the pillow so nice and straight across the top of the bed."

The only message we communicate by redoing their chores is that they never do anything right. If they have not already, they will soon quit trying to do something right. Constant criticism creates a rebellious spirit and will keep them from attempting to learn new activities, because they will think, "Whatever I do it is never good enough."

❧ *They will become discouraged with the work and it will not be done. (Nehemiah 6:9)*
❧ *Study and be eager and do your utmost to present yourself to God approved (tested by trial), a workman who has no cause to be ashamed. (2 Timothy 2:15 AMP)*

4. I do not force my kids to do chores because once they leave home they'll never be carefree again. My husband says I am reneging on one of my parental responsibilities. Could he be right?

*O*ne primary task we have as parents is to prepare our children to face adulthood with adequate survival skills. It is part of the command to us in Proverbs to train our children. When we let them grow up carefree (as you designate it), we are really encouraging laziness. As adults, they will be less effective in the job market than if they have been trained to understand that work is an integral part of life. It is common for kids to balk at doing chores, but this discontentment is more easily conquered when they are young than as adults. In fact, if allowed to flourish, it will be a battle they will wage all their life. Interestingly, I have known adults who become angry with their parents because they were not taught skills that would help them face adult independence.

There's a big difference between working your children like an adult and assigning age-appropriate responsibilities to them, increasing the load as they mature. Not only is performing chores vital to their maturity, it will make them better mates than if they were to go into a marriage expecting their spouse to care for them as Mom did.

Finally, nothing helps children's self-esteem more than knowing they are capable people. One way you can encourage their industry is to pay them for extra chores that they do. I'd encourage you to pay them well, too, as that will give credence to the viability of their work.

∾ *A wise son brings joy to his father, but a foolish son grief to his mother. (Proverbs 10:1 NIV)*
∾ *Do not merely look out for your own personal interests, but also for the interests of others. (Philippians 2:4)*

5. Our son is interested in a career in athletics. As a school-age student, the team he wants to play on has the majority of its games on Sunday. Should I allow him to participate in sports on our Sabbath?

There are several principles involved in making your decision. The injunction "Remember the Sabbath day to keep it Holy," is still a viable principle for us today. But Jesus also reminded the Pharisees that Sabbath was made for the man, not man for the Sabbath. If professional athletics is going to be his career choice, start now to incorporate the principles he will need. Find another day of the week for your son to set aside for worship. Some churches have Saturday night services, which might be an option. Encourage him to join a midweek Bible study.

You might also appeal to the sporting association leaders (just as Daniel did when he was offered the king's lavish food, Daniel 8). Poll other parents and see if they would like the games on another day. Present your view as a group. Just because it is current practice does not mean it has to remain so.

∾ *For I desire mercy, not sacrifice, and acknowledgment of God rather than burnt offerings. (Hosea 6:6 NIV)*
∾ *Jesus said to them, "The Sabbath was made for man, and not man for the Sabbath." (Mark 2:27)*

∼

6. Are there any foolproof methods we can implement to make sure our kids remain sexually pure before marriage?

There aren't any "fool-proofs" for children. However, if it is important to you and you demonstrate it by communicating it openly, you will have a greater chance of them incorporating the same belief into their value system.

An important point to remember when raising children is that if it is important to you, you need to make it a part of your everyday conversation. When situations arise in TV shows that reflect unchristian lifestyles, speak up and tell them why that behavior is unbiblical. When you speak about men and women in permanent relationships, speak of them as husband and wife. Talk about standards for dating and sexual purity from the time they are small. In this way it will become a part of their emotional/decisional fabric. That is how you reinforce what you consider important.

An idea we incorporated in our family is to give them a purity ring. When your teens are thirteen or fourteen years of age, on a predetermined birthday but before they are old enough to begin dating, get dressed up and take them to the restaurant of their choice. During dinner, speak to them again about the importance of remaining sexually pure in their thoughts and actions. Stress that sexual purity is a gift to God and the person they will someday marry.

Afterward, present them with a special ring to wear on their ring finger. During their wedding ceremony, some future day, they will present it to their spouse as a token of their purity and exchange it for their wedding ring. For more information, you can check with your local Christian bookstore, as they will have information on companies that produce specially engraved rings.

∾ *How can a young man keep his way pure? By keeping it according to Your word. (Psalms 119:9)*
∾ *You are to abstain from . . . sexual immorality. (Acts 15:29 NIV)*

7. My daughter is in love with a man who is not a believer, and I sense he is going to propose soon. What do I say to her? What position should I play, or is it my place to say anything?

I am assuming that your daughter is of legal age. You will get only one shot at this, so choose a time that is not stressful and prepare, beforehand, what you wish to say. Speak to her nonconfrontationally about your concerns. You might explain to her that a good marriage is a result of many factors, one of which is being able to share the same philosophy of life. As a believer, she already understands that God is her source for everything. When difficulties come, He is the one she goes to for help and support. However, since her fiancé's philosophy does not match hers, stress will inevitably result.

Use the following illustration to share that the intimacy she is hoping for will not occur without a spiritual connection: Draw a triangle on a piece of paper. Label the apex of it God, and place her name and her fiancé's on each of the two bottom corners. Explain that in order for true love to bring us closer together, we have to bring God into our relationship. As we each draw closer to God, demonstrated by moving up the sides of the triangle, the result is that each partner in the marriage also draws closer to each other.

Keep in mind that she will remember everything you say, and that should she marry him you do not want to say words that will make a breach between you. After you've spoken, the rest of your talk will be to God in prayer. Finally, hang onto your hope no matter what decision she reaches. God's decision to love her and her husband has been since the foundation of the world. He will continue to woo both of them, drawing them toward Him. You can rest upon that truth.

∾ *They were from nations about which the Lord had told the Israelites, "You must not intermarry with them, because they will surely turn your hearts after their gods." (1 Kings 11:2 NIV)*

✍ *Do not be yoked together with unbelievers. (2 Corinthians 6:14 NIV)*

~

8. Every teenage girl has a crush on movie stars, but I feel like my daughter's fascination is getting out of hand. She buys every movie, poster, and enters every contest in the teen magazines. Is this a phase that will pass?

*I*t is hard to find a balance between what we know is a foolish pastime and allowing our kids to express themselves in age-appropriate ways. But I understand your concern and believe you can speak to her regarding them. After discussing your concerns about her preoccupation with teenage idols, reach a compromise by using these guidelines:

Designate one wall, bulletin board, or notebook for her heartthrobs. When it gets full, she must toss something out to make room for the new trophies.

All pictures must pass mother's "modesty test" (something that will surely disbar quite a few of them). Explain to her that revealing photos of women are demeaning and help strengthen stereotypes about women being interesting only if they are sexy. It is especially important for young girls who are facing peer pressure to understand that the real person she is lies within, not in her appearance. Helping her gain acceptance and enjoyment of who she is will inoculate her from destructive habits some people indulge in to gain acceptance.

Give her alternatives. Introduce her to Christian substitutes. For example instead of buying a copy of *CosmoGirl*, introduce her to *Brio* magazine. It is a wonderful Christian magazine for girls, available from Focus on the Family (and *Breakaway* is for boys).

To help you know what's out there and to better prepare you when speaking to your teens, order a subscription to *Plugged In* magazine. It can tell you who are the Christian equivalents of popular musicians. For example, if she likes Britney Spears, you could buy her a CD of Jessica Simpson or Jaci Velasquez. *Plugged In* gives overviews of music, magazines, videos, and games in the marketplace. One idea I've heard parents doing is to confront their teens regarding the unwholesome music they listen to. They offer to purchase a new CD of an acceptable artist if they'll throw away the unacceptable ones and promise not to buy their products again.

You need to be aware of the influence of peer pressure in young teens' lives. To help combat their negative influence, get her involved in lots of wholesome activities: An energetic church youth group, scouting, and sports will bring her in contact with teens who have other perspectives and, I hope, a more wholesome focus for their attention, which will help realign hers.

One final opinion: Introduce her to good literature. There are wonderful biographies retelling the lives of magnificent Christians. Good literature will introduce her to other worlds that are real and in which people made a difference. It will broaden her horizons and reinforce the validity of God in her life. (See the bibliography for some suggested titles.)

∞ *You shall have no other gods before me. (Exodus 20:3)*
∞ *For where your treasure is, there your heart will be also. (Matthew 6:21)*

~

9. **Because I feel I had too much freedom as a child, I've raised my children rather strictly. I do not allow them to watch any secular movies or listen to secular music. Recently**

I've discovered that in the youth group parties, they have been participating in some of these banned activities. I do not want them to feel left out, but I do not want to compromise important training. How should I handle this situation?

*Y*ou have a right to expect the youth group to *help* you raise your kids, not create friction. Your first action should be to speak to the youth leaders, because you may not have the whole story. Your kids may be taking license without the leader's permission.

However, it has been my experience that those of us who are conservative Christian parents sometimes try to control our kids too tightly as they mature. Therefore, you may wish to re-evaluate your rules. With your children verging on young adulthood, you may find areas of compromise that you can accept. It is rare that our kids emulate everything we believe—as a matter of fact, I am wary of those who do because I believe they haven't worked our their own code of standards yet. If you can see that your object in the early years is to set the standard, in the middle years to help them set their own standards with your help, and then release them to be accountable to God on their own, you will have fulfilled your responsibility. Holding our children tightly can create rebellion, while gradually releasing them will help avoid it.

ꙮ *Hear, my son, your father's instruction and do not forsake your mother's teaching. (Proverbs 1:8)*
ꙮ *Fathers, do not provoke your children to anger, but bring them up in the discipline and instruction of the Lord. (Ephesians 6:4)*

10. My kids are often bored. Do you have any suggestions on how to entertain them?

*T*eaching children to entertain themselves is a skill that will benefit them their entire life. Ultimately it grows out of encouraging their interests and talents. If you demonstrate enjoyment in living, pursue hobbies, and interact with people, they will more naturally learn to find ways to occupy their time. To get them started, give them suggestions of things they could do. Use their God-given imagination and inquisitiveness to show them how to make up games. Help them learn a craft or hobby. Keep lots of books available for them to look through and read. You should be a resource to them, not responsible for their enjoyment. By not teaching them to take the initiative, you will wear yourself out before they start school.

Bored children are unchallenged children. Think about whether you do things for them that they are capable of learning to do for themselves. When they are challenged to learn and do new things, their enthusiasm for life will grow.

Sometimes boredom stems from laziness. If it becomes an ongoing problem, I would find a chore for them to do. That way they will think twice before they allow their mouths to form the syllables, "Mom, I am bored."

꙳ *In all labor there is profit. (Proverbs 14:23)*
꙳ *Conduct yourselves with wisdom. (Colossians 4:5)*

꙳

11. My three children argue all the time and always have. What can I do to bring peace to my home?

*T*here isn't a black-and-white answer to this question, because people who dwell together long-term tend to get on each other's nerves. You need to evaluate the degree of arguing, pinpoint the hot spots, and time the recurrences. If it is on-again/off-again verbal sparring without destructive language and does not escalate into violence, ignore it. You do need to make it clear that you will not tolerate name-calling or physical violence, and when these occur, hand out equal punishment immediately.

I am personally convinced that a lot of quarreling is an outgrowth of boredom. They do not know what to do with themselves and therefore they pick on each other. So, to curtail that, every time they quarrel, assign them a chore to do separately. It will amaze you how quickly they will pick up on what you are doing and learn to resolve differences amicably.

Second, teach them mediation skills and that they need to make peace with others. If you settle every argument, they will draw you into their pettiness each time. Place the responsibility back on the ones who are quarrelling. The home teaches us our first lessons in resolving conflict.

If one child in particular seems to be provoking more of the quarrels, set aside time to talk with him or her to find what is causing the behavior. Frustration stemming from a misperception about their place in the family can fuel many quarrels.

Finally, you set the emotional tone of your home. If you calmly deal with conflict, they will learn to reflect your peacefulness. Pray that your home will be a peaceful haven to all who enter it.

∾ *Wisdom has built her house. (Proverbs 9:1)*
∾ *What causes fights and quarrels among you? Don't they come from your desires that battle within you? (James 4:1)*

∾

12. I recall my school years with dread. What can I do to help my child do well in the school environment, emotionally and academically?

First of all, make sure you don't project your own negative feelings about school onto your children. They may enjoy school very much and your fears will be groundless. Your best contribution will be to provide a safe, nurturing home. When they know that home is a safe retreat at the end of each day, they can better cope with whatever problems they encounter during the day. Mary Pipher, in the July 1997 issue of *Current Thoughts & Trends,* cites a study that shows that kids who avoid behavioral problems generally have these factors in common:

- They come from a two-parent home.
- The family eats meals together regularly.
- They worship together as a family.
- They have fun together.

Teach your children the value of Christian behavior, such as kindness and friendliness. Make sure they understand that God is watching over them, not only for protection but accountability. In this way they may avoid giving in to wrong peer pressure. And do not make school the center of their life, but involve them in wholesome activities such as sports, scouts, and church youth groups in order to keep school's expectations from exerting too much pressure on them.

To help them do their best academically, create a learning environment. Choose the same time and place for study each day. If they do not have any homework, then insist they bring a book and read during that time. If you choose the dining-room table, it will allow you to oversee their activities and be available for help while cooking dinner. Make sure there are resources available, such as a dictionary and newspapers. The common denominator for good students seems to be reading competency, so fill your home with good books to encourage reading. Be a role model by being a reader yourself. Make trips to the library a weekly part of your schedule. Keep in touch with their teachers so they will feel free to contact you at soon as academic problems arise.

❧ *Teach them to your children, talking about them when you sit at home and when you walk along the road, when you lie down and when you get up. (Deuteronomy 11:19)*
❧ *Be diligent to present yourself approved to God as a workman who does not need to be ashamed, accurately handling the word of truth. (2 Timothy 2:15)*

~

13. My fifteen-year-old daughter is anticipating her first group date. I want to talk to her but do not want to suggest something she may not have thought of first. What should I discuss with her?

If she's fifteen then no doubt all of her thoughts are concentrated on dating and the boys she is hoping will ask her out. You have a right and a responsibility to help your daughter set standards for dating. One principle you can encourage her to implement is found in Song of Solomon (2:7), which entreats us to not awaken love too quickly. Encourage her to guard her heart and protect it for the one special man she will marry. When you speak to her about the facts of life, explain to her that sexual attraction, once aroused, is hard to deny, so persuade her to delay all physical expressions such as hand-holding and kissing for several years. Discuss her options if she gets into uncomfortable circumstances. Some other specific areas you might cover are:

• Isolation: She and her date should not leave the party or go off by themselves. They must remain with the group at all times.
• Rehearse with her what she will say when (if) offered

something illegal such as drugs, cigarettes, or alcohol.

• Always know what adults will be present and exactly where the teenagers are going. Ask the title of the movie.

• Role-play what her response will be if her date tries to do anything that makes her feel uncomfortable.

• Always make sure she has money for a phone call (or carries a cell phone) and assure her that you or her dad will never be angry at having to come and rescue her. Cell phones still have a certain cachet to them, which makes an electronic leash not seem like a hindrance to a teenager's freedom but gives parents great peace of mind.

• Make it a rule that the boy must come in to the house and meet you and her father. The best deterrent to improper behavior toward your daughter will be the knowledge her date will carry of Dad knowing him and where he lives. Also, it is perfectly proper for Dad to verbalize his expectations to the young man that he will act like a gentleman while with her.

Finally, while she is still in group dating, you may wish to introduce her to the concept of nondating. This is a school of thought that is growing among many Christian young people. They have come to realize that the dating scene is not adequately preparing them for marriage. They see that the usual outcome of casual dating results in negative emotional effects and does little to increase communication skills between a man and woman. Instead they are opting to work on friendships in groups, leaving God to direct them into a lasting relationship in His time. For more information, see the bibliography listing of the book *I Kissed Dating Goodbye*.

If you will make teaching values a part of your everyday life, then each new stage will not be so traumatic for everyone. Seize all teachable moments that come your way: When a TV program demonstrates a situation that is questionable, ask your kids, "Do you agree with his/her choice?"

And in closing, we always gave permission to our kids to

make their parents the "bad guys." So when they encountered situations or suggestions they knew they should not go along with, but felt unable to state it strongly enough for themselves, they were more than welcome to say, "My mom and dad won't let me."

∾ *How can a young person stay pure? By obeying your word and following its rules. (Psalms 119:9 NLT)*
∾ *Pray for us, for we are sure that we have a good conscience, desiring to conduct ourselves honorably in all things. (Hebrews 13:18)*

∾

14. I am a single mom who must work full-time. How can I make sure my kids are trained biblically?

*A*s a single parent, you have one of the hardest jobs in the entire world. You come home from work exhausted and sometimes emotionally unable to meet your kids' needs. But God has provided tools to help you carry this load. The first thing you should do is find a good Bible-teaching church with strong children/teen programs. A caring church family will provide all sorts of emotional help to you in the coming years. They will reinforce your values and provide outlets for frustration and energy. Be open with the leadership about needing mentors and support, and hold them accountable as the Body of Christ to provide this to your family.

The bottom line in raising children is to show them the way to God. If you fall short in every other area, which won't happen, but instill in them a relationship with God or even the knowledge of how much God loves them and how to approach Him, you have given them the fundamental cornerstone of life. Along with that, teach them to revere God. For when a child knows he is accountable not only to Mom (who may not see everything) but ultimately to God (who never misses anything), he will think twice before lying, stealing, and committing other common juvenile crimes. It makes everything else easier to teach and many lessons will be unnecessary.

You also need to give yourself grace. Every parent falls short of the standard we set in our mind for ourselves and gets discouraged. It is impossible to maintain your status quo for two decades. When you are down, just fall into Jesus' arms and allow His love to refresh you.

∽ *By wisdom a house is built, and by understanding it is established; and by knowledge the rooms are filled with all precious and pleasant riches. (Proverbs 24:3, 4)*
∽ *Pay close attention to yourself and to your teaching; persevere in these things, for as you do this you will ensure salvation both for yourself and for those who hear you. (1 Timothy 4:16)*

~

15. I am a single mother with three school-age children. I have a college degree but still struggle financially each month to support myself and my kids. My ex-husband, the kids' father, lives in town and makes a very good income, but has refused to pay any of his court-ordered child support. How wrong would it be for me to sue him for back support?

I may be going out on a biblical limb with my answer, but I do believe that if suing is the only way to get the necessary finances to support your children, then do it. God made both you and him responsible as caregivers for your children, and unless he is legitimately unemployed, he needs to accept his part of the responsibility. Before you consult a lawyer though, talk to your state Department of Health and Welfare. The government is getting involved in finding deadbeat dads.

130

If you qualify, they will go after your husband for the money, collect it, and pay it to you without you having to get involved in anything that could be unpleasant.

∾ *Cursed is the man who withholds justice from the alien, the fatherless or the widow. Then all the people shall say, "Amen!" (Deuteronomy 27:19 NIV)*
∾ *But if anyone does not provide for his own, and especially for those of his household, he has denied the faith and is worse than an unbeliever. (1 Timothy 5:8)*

∼

16. How can I instill in my kids the daily habit of reading the Bible and praying without turning them off religion altogether?

I am not sure that you need to be particularly concerned with the outcome, but concentrate on your responsibility before God. You can try to teach it in a manner in which they will see the benefits in their lives, but even if they do not, it does not follow that you shouldn't have taught them. I do not think God holds us responsible for the decisions our children make regarding the truth we've taught them, He just holds us responsible to be obedient to his commands. Once again, the important factor is whether your life demonstrates the importance of spending time with God every day. Do you consider it important enough to carve out three to five minutes each day to gather the family for family altar? (Hint: Dinnertime is a wonderful time.) Albert Schweitzer, the great humanitarian, said, "Example is not the main thing in influencing others. It is the only thing."

Some practical ways you can encourage your children spiritually are (see the bibliography for places to order the items listed) the following.

- Age-appropriate Bibles
- One-year Bibles—they have them for teens
- Bible videos and tapes
- CD Bible or GameBoy Bible (our elementary-aged son loved taking his GameBoy to church and reading the Scriptures on it)
- A colorful blank book for journaling
- A book of prayers

∾ *These words, which I am commanding you today, shall be on your heart. You shall teach them diligently to your sons and shall talk of them when you sit in your house and when you walk by the way and when you lie down and when you rise up. (Deuteronomy 6:7)*

∾ *For I am mindful of the sincere faith within you, which first dwelt in your grandmother Lois, and your mother Eunice, and I am sure that it is in you as well. (2 Timothy 1:5)*

⁓

17. I am determined to be a good Christian parent and provide my children with a stable, happy childhood. I am sure God honors my determination, but I am discovering that I am feeling anxious and fearful all the time. What is wrong with me?

You may be setting perfection as your standard and believe being perfect is achievable. In other words, *you* are going to be a good Christian parent and *you* are going to give your children a stable, happy childhood.

What is missing is that you are leaving out the most important aspect of being a parent—the knowledge that you cannot do it on your own. You need God to come beside you to accomplish this most important mission of your life.

If you will practice leaning on God, you will find that

your stress level will decrease in direct proportion to your dependency on His wisdom for your children. When everything depends on "us," we're in trouble. Instead, realize that while you have a responsibility to raise these precious gifts He has entrusted to you, it requires His wisdom and strength to complete the job. Switch your focus from your performance to God's provision. You will need His care, insight, protection, strength, and encouragement every day of your life. Instead of trying to give your child a perfect childhood, concentrate on giving her Eternal Life by introducing her to Jesus. Being a parent is not a one-time event but a lifelong adventure. Christian author Ruth Vaughn says, "Parenthood is a partnership with God. You are not molding iron nor chiseling marble; you are working with the Creator of the universe in shaping human character and determining destiny."

Anytime you feel fear overcoming you, stop and place everything (the day, the situation, the circumstance) in God's hand, and thank Him for taking care of it.

∾ *All your sons will be taught of the LORD; and the well-being of your sons will be great. (Isaiah 54:13)*
∾ *For I know whom I have believed and I am convinced that He is able to guard what I have entrusted to Him until that day. (2 Timothy 1:12)*

∼

18. My kids are always wanting to have their friends over. They fill the house, empty the refrigerator, and generally leave me little peace and quiet. How should I suggest they go to someone else's house sometimes?

You are lucky! Kids are very perceptive about where they are wanted, and they will not go where they are uncomfortable. The best gift you can give your children is to provide a welcoming home for them and their friends. I know it is untidy and noisy, but I assure you when they are out of the nest and gone you'll miss the hubbub that they brought. The easiest way to know what's going on in their lives is to have them bring home their friends. Just by passing through the rooms you will gain information that you would not otherwise. I understand there is a fine line between eavesdropping and snooping and a lack of trust toward a teen may precipitate rebellion. However, being a peripheral part of their interactions allows you to keep abreast of who they are hanging out with and give input (along with the popcorn and cookies) into everyday decisions they are dealing with.

I grew up in a casual, happy family of five kids. My parents, who were struggling financially, still made it a point to buy a case of boxed pizzas each month. Every Sunday night after church the teens in our congregation assembled at our home for pizza, soda, and lots of fun. My parents did it because they wanted to offer us an alternative place to socialize than the local unsupervised teenage hangouts.

However, you do not have to allow them to consume your food budget every week. Find cheap food that is filling and stock up on that. Call it the "free" food, meaning they are allowed to eat all they want of it, and make the rest of the refrigerator off limits. Some suggestions are: popcorn, sliced veggies, Top Ramen. You can mix up large batches of peanut butter cookie dough and freeze it in cartons in the fridge. When they come in hungry after school they can scoop it out and bake hot, fragrant cookies. Naturally, the choices involving the stove would only be allowed when your kids reach adolescence.

With a little forethought you can still be the official mess hall and survive financially, too. Consider where you kids could be congregating if your home wasn't open, and offer up a prayer of thanks that they'll come. The peace of mind is worth the cost of the extra groceries.

By wisdom a house is built, and by understanding it is established. (Proverbs 24:3)

Be hospitable to one another without complaint. (1 Peter 4:9)

~

19. I am so tired of carpooling. How can I convince my husband to buy a used car for the kids to carry themselves back and forth to school and other appointments?

A car is a tremendous blessing for moms. First of all, for some reason kids will talk in a car more freely. Maybe it is because your attention isn't fully on them, it is on the road, and that makes them feel it is safe to speak. I have also noticed that when they have friends along, each will speak about issues and feelings in a way that will inform you how they are doing and give you information you'd never get otherwise.

In a car they are your captive audience. If you want to ask them about something or gauge their reaction to a situation, you can do it because where are they going to go? I encourage you to see the potential you have in car time and consider it a blessing, not a burden.

However, understanding your undoubtedly busy schedule, I am sure you could work out a system with your husband in which he is able to share the transportation burden. It may be that he can assume all car-pooling obligations that need to be done in the evenings, leaving you free to fix dinner and clean up afterward.

We will not conceal them from their children, but tell to the generation to come the praises of the Lord, and His strength and His wondrous works that He has done. (Psalms 78:4)

Rejoice always; pray without ceasing; in everything give thanks; for this is God's will for you in Christ Jesus. (1 Thessalonians 5:16–18)

20. I always thought that if I had a good relationship with my child, I didn't need to worry about him committing suicide. But the nice teen living two doors down from us, from a good family whom we've known for several years, committed suicide last week. Not only is the family reeling from the shock, we are too. Can you tell me what would prompt this?

*Y*our premise is a good one because, for the most part, strong relationships will keep most teens from falling off the edge and into dangerous behaviors. When someone takes his or her own life, the tsunami of guilt that washes over everyone left behind is devastating because we never get to know what it was that finally drove her or him over the edge.

Some information I can give you to start with comes from the American Academy of Child & Adolescent Psychiatry. They list these symptoms, as warning signs of adolescents who may try to kill themselves:

- Change in eating and sleeping habits
- Withdrawal from friends, family, and regular activities
- Violent actions, rebellious behavior, or running away
- Drug and alcohol use
- Unusual neglect of personal appearance
- Marked personality change
- Persistent boredom, difficulty concentrating, or a decline in the quality of schoolwork
- Frequent complaints about physical symptoms, often related to emotions, such as stomachaches, headaches, fatigue, etc.
- Loss of interest in pleasurable activities
- Not tolerating praise or rewards

One last thought: My sister, who is a nurse, stressed the importance of knowing any side effects of the medication teens are taking. She says there is an acne medicine that in recent years has been linked to suicide. So, very carefully read the cautions that come with all the prescriptions your family takes.

> *For he who finds me finds life. (Proverbs 8:35)*
> *For out of the heart come evil thoughts, murders, adulteries, fornications, thefts, false witness, slanders. (Matthew 15:19)*

~

21. My twenty-one-year-old daughter is so anxious to fall in love, I am concerned she will accept the first man to show her any attention. How can I communicate her vulnerability to her?

When "spring comes and young men's thoughts turn to love" (along with young women), your words probably aren't going to penetrate. I would certainly make it a matter of prayer, asking God to protect and guide her. Second, I'd analyze the quality of her life. Does she have good friends who enjoy being active? If all she does is go to work and maybe to the movies, the scope of her life is too limited. This allows her time to brood over what she sees as life's inequities. You can suggest night classes in an area she has expressed interest or the goal of a great vacation. If she is very open about wanting a man, you may be able to offer her direction. Speak to her about where she is spending her time. Does it bring her into contact with suitable men? Does she belong to a college-age youth group, a sports group, or volunteer somewhere regularly?

Sometimes young women think they need to be married because many of their friends are—the age-old "grass is greener on the other side of the fence" school of thought. This may be brought on by not having developed sufficient interests for their own life. If you can expand the borders of her world to see other opportunities in which she can become involved, she may not feel such an urgency to get married.

∾ *Hope deferred makes the heart sick, but desire fulfilled is a tree of life. (Proverbs 13:12)*
∾ *Let her marry. (1 Corinthians 7:36)*

∼

22. Our income does not allow us to give expensive gifts or exotic vacations to our kids. I am concerned that they will not have happy memories of their childhood. How can we compensate for the lack in their lives?

The Bible's emphasis is on spiritual and eternal values. From this perspective, lack of money is not often viewed as a detriment. The amount of money we spend on our children is not what is important. The important thing is that we create memories for them.

Because you are not affluent is not a reason for guilt or to feel that you have deprived them of something. They have less money than their peers—so what? Many people raised in very affluent circumstances testify to their poor upbringing because all they had was money. If you concentrate on building a solid family where they feel loved, accepted, and then throw in goodly amounts of fun, you will be successful.

On the other hand, special treats such as vacations do not have to break the bank. There is camping in our great national forests, visiting relatives, and going to places of interest that are either free or low in fees. My sister and her family spent one summer, when finances were very low, taking a vacation at home. She and her husband planned all sorts of sightseeing activities in their city. They took the city bus to points of interest, and when they came home they didn't do housework but rather played games and just generally hung out together all week. It didn't cost much, but the memories were priceless.

When our parents celebrated their fortieth wedding anniversary, each of the five children in my family spoke about our childhood memories. Unbeknownst to each other, with no prior planning, we each commented on the family vacations we took each summer—seven people crammed into a 1957 Rambler sedan. It had no air conditioning and much of the time was spent alongside the road waiting for the engine to cool down so we could continue on the journey, but all we remembered was how much fun it was. Concentrate on making memories; do not worry about the lack of money for them. Be creative!

꙾ *Each of you is to take up a stone on his shoulder, according to the number of the tribes of the Israelites, to serve as a sign among you. In the future, when your children ask you, "What do these stones mean?" tell them that the flow of the Jordan was cut off before the ark of the covenant of the LORD. When it crossed the Jordan, the waters of the Jordan were cut off. These stones are to be a memorial to the people of Israel forever. (Joshua 4:5–7)*

꙾ *So then, brothers, stand firm and hold to the teachings we passed on to you, whether by word of mouth or by letter. (2 Thessalonians 2:15)*

~

23. My mother-in-law criticizes us for allowing our children to argue with us. We think she is overreacting and expecting too much from preschoolers.

*E*very generation believes that the next generation is too lenient with their children. Therefore, she may or may not be expecting too much of young children. It does take a long time to raise children and that is why God gives them to us for a minimum of eighteen years.

However, establishing that Mom and Dad are in charge is a vital lesson for the health of your family. Allowing small children to argue with you before you have established who's in charge will lead to chaos. When they are very young, it is perfectly okay for you to ask your child to do something and expect them to obey you without any question. Democracy only works when the limits have been established, so you need to demonstrate that Mom and Dad are to be obeyed.

However, for your child never to be allowed to question your decisions is also wrong. As a rule of thumb, the younger the child, the less they need to question your direction.

To illustrate how flexibility works into discipline, visualize a boxing ring. The corner posts of a ring are rigid and do not allow flexibility. They can be likened to early childhood when your goal should be to teach your children to listen and obey. You need to feel confident that in an emergency, should you call your child, he or she will respond instead of saying, "Just a minute." However, if you travel from the corner posts along the ropes, you will notice they become more lax and there is give in them. While they will continue to keep you within the safety of the ring, they also allow more freedom. This area can be likened to older childhood and adolescence. Once your child accepts your authority, you can begin to allow him or her to query your decisions and explore other options that may be open. In this way, you have taught your child the importance of his opinion while still respecting your leadership. There is a fine line between an argumentative versus a questioning attitude. Your children's tone of voice will be one clue. Their acceptance of your final decision is still another indication.

❧ *A youngster's heart is filled with foolishness, but discipline will drive it away. (Proverbs 22:15 NLT)*

∾ *Fathers, do not provoke your children to anger, but bring them up in the discipline and instruction of the Lord. (Ephesians 6:4)*

∾

24. We have friends who refuse to allow their kids to celebrate Halloween, insisting it is a pagan holiday. Don't you feel they are going to force their kids to rebel?

*I*t depends on how they handle it and with what they replace it. I understand people not wishing their kids to celebrate spookiness and the occult, especially if he or she is sensitive and easily frightened. I do emphasize, though, that whenever you take something away from your child that is an accepted part of their peers' enjoyment, you would be wise to replace it with something better. Now, I know that some of you are thinking, "Prayer meeting! What could be better!" To a child, that is not an acceptable alternative. It is not an acceptable alternative to me, either. Your substitute activity needs to be able to carry an equal weight in the competition. Can you provide a Harvest Party for your children and their friends without anything spooky? Can you host a Bible costume party for them? Many things trigger rebellion, but alienation is a strong factor in young people. You need to give them ammunition so that when they return to school after the holiday, and everyone is talking about how much fun they had, they will be able to say, "Wait until you hear what I did!"

∾ *A wise man is cautious and turns away from evil, but a fool is arrogant and careless. (Proverbs 14:16)*
∾ *Finally, brethren, whatever is true, whatever is honorable, whatever is right, whatever is pure, whatever is lovely, whatever is of good repute, if there is any excellence and if anything worthy of praise, dwell on these things. (Philippians 4:8)*

25. My second-grader seems to lie for no reason. Is it just a phase for attention and should I ignore it?

Except for very young children, no wrong behavior should be ignored. That does not mean that every infraction needs severe punishment, either. Does she lie by telling "stories," which are simply an indication of a creative imagination? She may not know the difference between pretend and real. Therefore, you may need to do some explaining about what is pretend—things she thinks up that come from her imagination, and things that really happened. If most of her lying occurs in this manner, help her find a way to explain that it is pretend, before she tells the story. Once you know she understands the difference, begin calling her on it whenever you hear it. You can say, "But that is just pretend, isn't it?"

If she is lying to avoid punishment, that is a different issue. Begin by asking her if she knows what lying is. Have her tell you, without you putting words in her mouth, just so you will know if she understands. Point out that when we lie, we make Jesus very sad; plus it makes Mom and Dad sad, too. Tell her you are going to help her recognize her lies by making her sit in the corner for five minutes (or whatever punishment your family uses) each time she does it. Link lying to its spiritual root by praying about it each day with her, asking Jesus to help her be truthful.

∾ *For my mouth will speak truth. (Proverbs 8:7 NKJV)*
∾ *But speaking the truth in love. (Ephesians 4:15)*

~

26. If it only takes love to make a family, why shouldn't homosexual couples be allowed to be foster parents? Isn't it more important that children have loving adults to care for them?

*T*here is some truth in the statement. It does take love to make a family, but love is only one ingredient in the recipe of a family. It is important to ask ourselves why families were formed and who formed them. God set in order families, assigning basic responsibilities for fathers and mothers. They are for:

- Fathers to teach (Deuteronomy 6:7)
- Mothers to train (Proverbs 22:6)
- Fathers to provide for their physical needs (II Corinthians 12:14)
- Mothers to nurture children (Ephesians 6:4)
- Fathers to give direction and leadership (I Timothy 3:4)
- Both fathers and mothers to love (Titus 2:4)

This basic Judeo-Christian thinking has been the basis of all law, government, and social order in civilized societies since biblical times.

Regarding allowing homosexual couples to be foster parents: There has not been enough scientific research done on homosexual adoption to make an informed conclusion as to how it will impact children. We would be unwise to make radical societal changes that would affect our most vulnerable members of society without more scientific data. A report in the July 28, 2002, issue of the *Pentecostal Evangel* cites that sociologist Patricia Morgan, author of *Children as Trophies*, gives four reasons that the often-cited studies purporting positive influence of homosexual adoption are invalid:

- Predetermines expected outcomes
- Uses self-selected volunteers
- Relies on small, nonrandom samples
- Conclusions reached do not fit the data

The rationale for accepting a standard of behavior should be whether or not it aligns with Scripture. Dr. James Dobson, in

Solid Answers, is quoted as saying, "If the term family refers to any group of people who love each other, then the term ceases to have meaning. In that case, five homosexual men can be a 'family' until one feels unloved and then there are four. Under such a definition, one man and six women could be regarded as a legal entity, reintroducing the debate over polygamy."

As Christians, we are called to uphold God's Word. Again, Dr. Dobson, in *Solid Answers*, defines the traditional definition of a family, following the precepts of Scripture, as "a group of individuals who are related to one another by marriage, birth, or adoption—nothing more, nothing else."

∾ *You shall not lie with a male as one lies with a female; it is an abomination. (Leviticus 18:22)*
∾ *But from the beginning of creation, God made them male and female. (Mark 10:6)*

~

27. If all fear is learned, and I've been very careful to make my toddler feel secure, why is he so afraid of the dark?

This is probably another area of popular thought that is not rooted in Scripture. While many fears are a learned response, not all of them are, since fear comes from Satan. It is part of his arsenal of weapons against us. And he can target children. Even before they understand about good and evil, you should be speaking God's truth to your children. One of the first Scriptures you can teach them is "When I am afraid, I will trust in You" (Psalms 56:3). By planting God's Word in their hearts at a very young age, you show them who they can depend on and place their confidence and trust in all their lives. When they express fear, begin to pray aloud, thanking Jesus for his protection and his love for us. Encouraging them to repeat your words teaches them to pray.

෴ *In peace I will both lie down and sleep, for You alone, O LORD, make me to dwell in safety. (Psalms 4:8)*
෴ *For God hath not given us the spirit of fear; but of power, and of love, and of a sound mind. (2 Timothy 1:7 KJV)*

~

28. Aren't we fooling ourselves to believe that the abstinence message will mean anything to hormone-driven teens?

I do not believe that because truth is not heeded it makes it unnecessary. I do believe though that abstinence alone isn't as good a message as adding the spiritual reason for abstinence. A much better deterrent is reminding them that we will all stand before God and give an account for ourselves and that includes transgressing His laws about sexual activity. Sometimes nothing keeps us on the right path other than the knowledge that we will answer for our behavior. Incorporating that knowledge into our kids' psyche is an important step in their ability to assume mature decision-making skills.

෴ *Who may ascend into the hill of the LORD? And who may stand in His holy place? He who has clean hands and a pure heart. (Psalms 24:3–4)*
෴ *If you keep yourself pure, you will be a utensil God can use for his purpose. Your life will be clean, and you will be ready for the Master to use you for every good work. (2 Timothy 2:21 NLT)*

~

29. I've heard about the practice of having family devotions. Our children are still small, so should we start now or wait until they are older and can better understand the Bible?

Every value that you feel is important for your children should be implemented as soon as possible. If they grow up with a practice being a normal part of family routine, you will not have a struggle convincing them of its importance when they are older. This works with scrubbing necks as well as attending church. I cannot stress too much, though, that devotions should be age-appropriate and *short*. The bottom line is to do it joyfully, regularly, and keep it from three to five minutes long. Some creative ways you can have devotions are:

- Read a short Bible story and say a family prayer at the supper table.
- Have the children act out a story and say a prayer together.
- As you tuck them into bed; you can sing songs about Jesus and pray.
- As they grow older you can add reading aloud a chapter of a biography of a prominent Christian such as Corrie ten Boom to enrich their lives.

Mothers may obsess over creating a perfect Christian family. Sometimes husbands don't catch the same vision in the same way and it may be that in your house Daddy is uncomfortable with the idea of leading a family altar. If your husband is resistant, do not make an issue of it. You and children can incorporate it into the bedtime routine or some other time you have together each day.

∽ *You shall teach them diligently to your sons and shall talk of them when you sit in your house and when you walk by the way and when you lie down and when you rise up. You shall bind them as a sign on your hand and they shall be as frontals on your forehead. You shall write them on the doorposts of your house and on your gates. (Deuteronomy 6:7–9)*
∽ *Teach and preach these principles. (1 Timothy 6:2)*

30. My husband is a good, hard-working man who seems to feel that our kids belong to me. He believes that since he earns the money, I should be responsible for everything else, including the children. I feel like I am drowning, emotionally, and wonder how can I make him see I need him to help?

While our husbands are the head of the family, God did not intend for you to be the sole nurturer and trainer of your children. Children are a heritage and it will take the input from both you and your husband to instill in them their sense of identity and purpose that is so important for success in life. Children are a joint responsibility.

You will need to bathe this situation in prayer. I imagine you've already discovered that he will not or cannot listen to you. Pray to God and ask him to soften your husband's heart and open his eyes. Pray also for a mentor for him. I imagine, without knowing your situation, that your husband is acting as a father in the way that he was raised. This is another situation that calls for an appeal. If you need the method refreshed for you, consult Question 20 in the section on marriage.

The generous man will be prosperous. (Proverbs 11:25)
I pray that the eyes of your heart may be enlightened. (Ephesians 1:18)

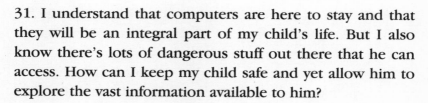

31. I understand that computers are here to stay and that they will be an integral part of my child's life. But I also know there's lots of dangerous stuff out there that he can access. How can I keep my child safe and yet allow him to explore the vast information available to him?

You are correct to understand that computers will only become more and more an integral part of our lives.

However, the Bible indicates that being discerning is an important aspect of acquiring knowledge. You are also right that there is much available that you would not want your kids to find. Blocking services that screen individual offensive sites are widely available. There are various Christian Internet companies that individually screen sites allowing you better searching options. For instance, they would allow you to search on breast cancer, where other services that block words without finding where they lead would not allow that search because of the word *breast*. As your kids mature, and school assignments increase, you may be forced to remove blocking in order for them to access research materials for classes. If you have been open with your kids and spoken to them regularly about guarding their eyes, lifting restrictions will be a natural step.

Furthermore, use these additional guidelines for computer/Internet in your home:

- Do not place the computer in an isolated part of the home. Keep it in areas you frequent to help your kids resist accessing forbidden sites.
- Do not allow anyone to have a secret password. All files must be available to the whole family.
- Have a computer-savvy friend show you how you can go "behind the scenes" and track the sites that have been visited from your computer.
- Do not allow your kids to give out their name, address, or phone number to *anyone* on the Internet.
- My personal opinion on chat rooms is that young children should never go into them, and that older children need constant supervision in theirs.
- Speak to your kids often about purity in thoughts. It is something we all need to be reminded of in this wicked age in which we live.

∾ *I will set no worthless thing before my eyes. (Psalms 101:3)*

~ *Finally, brethren, whatever is true, whatever is honorable, whatever is right, whatever is pure, whatever is lovely, whatever is of good repute, if there is any excellence and if anything worthy of praise, dwell on these things. (Philippians 4:8)*

~

32. How can my husband and I know which schooling decision is best for our children—public, private, or home?

No one method is the absolutely perfect method for everyone. The most important decision is one on which you and your spouse will agree. You are responsible to God for your children. It is true that the Bible indicates that the fathers are to be the ones who teach the children, but of course there were not schools available then. However, deciding to place your children in a school does not mean you are abdicating your responsibility, rather you are allowing someone to share in some of the training of your children, with yourselves as the final authority.

If you are considering home schooling, take a hard look at your family. Do you have a scheduled, disciplined household? Do your children listen to you and obey quickly? The parents who home school but fail to adequately educate their children usually do so because their home isn't under control. If you do not have your children on a regular schedule, adding school will only increase the chaos to the home. Furthermore, do you like to learn? You will be the role model who can open the world to your children or make them simply rote learners. If you are willing to spend time planning lessons and seeking creative ways to apply what is learned, you will probably find this a fulfilling option. See the bibliography for the homeschooling resource.

If you are considering a public school, go for an interview

with the principal. Ask her how open she is to your input. Will she give respect to your beliefs? When our oldest began kindergarten, we did not want her participating in some of the activities, and the school was gracious enough to provide alternatives for her. Ask about the school's curriculum. It was important to us whether the teacher would teach evolution as a theory or fact. Find out how the students have done on standardized achievement tests. Review the school manual thoroughly and ask about anything you do not understand.

When you are considering private schooling, ask if it is accredited. Can you afford the tuition or will it place a financial burden on the family? What additional expectations are given to the parents of the students? Does the private school have a religious affiliation with which you are comfortable? Are there carpools or busing from your area of town? If it will take several hours out of Mom's day delivering and retrieving the kids, it may not be worth it.

∾ *On the lips of the discerning, wisdom is found. (Proverbs 10:13)*
∾ *And this I pray, that your love may abound still more and more in real knowledge and all discernment. (Philippians 1:9)*

~

33. We have Christian friends who believe in the theory of evolution, which in turn really upsets other Christian friends in our group. I am wondering whether you believe Creationism versus evolution is really all that important?

What we believe is foundational to how we live. Perhaps your friends who say they believe in the theory of evolution are instead reacting to problems they see in the story of Creationism. In other words, they feel that the teaching of Creation as told in the Bible has a lot of gaps in it, which it does. They may feel that there is more to that story than what we read in Scripture, which is also true.

All through the Bible we are given enough information to proceed, but not always the whole story. God wishes us to come to Him in faith and to follow Him in faith and therefore He does not satisfy our curiosity on every point of contention.

However, your friends may not be honest with themselves if they say that they believe in the theory of evolution. Evolution is based upon random variation and natural selection. The process denies any intervention of a higher power, God. So if they are born-again Christians, by their decision to accept Christ's intervention in their life, they are demonstrating that they do not believe that life is lived simply by chance but by choice.

It is important for Christians to accept that God created the world; however, just how that occurred may be viewed in several ways. Some of us believe that He created the world in six 24-hour days. Others believe that He created the world in six days but view the days as in God's time: "A thousand years is as a day with God" (2 Peter 3:8). Third, some Christians believe that God created the world, but evolution was the process that He chose in which to do it. However, those who hold this view do believe that man was a special exception, in that God created man and they did not evolve from apes.

Of course, the greatest danger in believing in the theory of evolution is simply that to do so rules out the existence of God. Then it follows that since there is no God, there is no consequence to how I live my life.

∾ *Then the LORD God formed man of dust from the ground, and breathed into his nostrils the breath of life; and man became a living being. (Genesis 2:7)*

∾ *For now we see in a mirror dimly, but then face to face; now I know in part, but then I will know fully just as I also have been fully known. (1 Corinthians 13:12)*

HEALTH

1. If, as the Bible says, we're simply made of dust and to dust we'll return, does it really matter if I take care of my health? Besides, God has already numbered our days.

Yes, it does matter because whatever days He has allowed for you, they are to be used to glorify Him. Poor health will diminish your quality of life. I'm sure you agree that your ability to work for God and glorify Him in your body is severely restricted if, for instance, you are on a ventilator. We need to use every means given to us to worship God and to proclaim His goodness. Getting regular checkups, watching our weight, getting exercise, and refusing to indulge in unhealthy practices, such as smoking, will result in a life in which we can worship God. Quality of life increases when we take care of our health; and that in turn allows us to work for God. Finally, God desires good things for His children, including abundant life. Poor health is a terrible burden. Jesus paid a price for our healing with the stripes He took for us on his back and the suffering He endured on the cross. He desires you to be whole—body, soul, and spirit.

∞ *"For I will restore you to health and I will heal you of your wounds," declares the LORD. (Jeremiah 30:17)*
∞ *Beloved, I pray that in all respects you may prosper and be in good health, just as your soul prospers. (3 John 2)*

2. From the news it seems like the attack of germ warfare is a very real possibility. I am consumed with fear and have not had an undisturbed night's sleep since September 11, 2001.

For the first thirty years of my life, fear kept me in bondage. At age thirty, I had never spent a night alone in my life. I had either lived at home, with a roommate, or been married. So when Michael came home one day and announced that he would be gone six weeks that summer to counsel at youth camps, I was in turmoil. It was time to get serious about my phobia. It wasn't that I wasn't a Christian, because I was. It wasn't that I didn't believe God *could* keep me safe—I wasn't too sure He *would*. I had not placed my trust in His keeping power.

During that summer, I discovered the power of the sword. God's Word. I chose Psalm 4, verse 8 ("In peace and rest I will lie down and sleep for God keeps me safe."), as my weapon. When I went to bed at night, I spoke that verse out loud. If I woke up during the night (and I often did the first week), I immediately spoke that verse out loud again. I literally wielded the Word of God for the purpose that God gave it to us—to defend myself. During that summer (and yes, I survived all six weeks on my own), I learned the power of speaking the Word.

Every generation faces an unknown future. We can either ignore it by burying our head or face it with Someone who is not only here for us today, but will also be there tomorrow—God. I chose God. The refrain of an old gospel song by Ira Stanphill says it best: "Many things about tomorrow I don't seem to understand; but I know who holds tomorrow and I know who holds my hand."

Germ warfare may be a very real possibility—and maybe something even worse. Keeping your eyes on the "what ifs" will destroy your peace of mind (as it has already done). Instead keep your eyes on Jesus. He can give you peace beyond any comprehension.

When our eyes are on the circumstances, we leave the field open for Satan to play mind games with us. The only way to shut out his voice is to defeat it with the Word of God.

Besides memorizing Scriptures, some additional ways to find peace are:

• Guard your eye and ear gates. In other words, do not

bury your head; but do not sit in front of CNN all day long and listen to the tragedies taking place in the world.
- Fill your mind and heart with good Christian music.
- Play the Bible on Tape in your home as you go about your work.

❧ *God is our refuge and strength, a very present help in trouble. Therefore, we will not fear, though the earth should change and though the mountains slip into the heart of the sea. (Psalms 46:1–2)*

❧ *For God has not given us a spirit of fear and timidity, but of power, love and self-discipline. (2 Timothy 1:7 NLT)*

~

3. My friend disapproves of my occasional cigarette, insisting that smoking is sinful. But she does not agree when I say that her overeating is against God's Commandments, too.

I know the temptation is great, but do not keep trying to win this difference of opinion. The subject cannot be won by either side, for each habit causes serious health problems. It is pointless to rate sin. When we miss the mark by mistreating our body, which God says is where the Holy Spirit dwells, it is wrong. No matter whether we mistreat it via drugs, smoking, or gluttony, the end result is that we are violating God's wishes and "dirtying up" the living house of God.

Speaking for myself, I too have been guilty of categorizing sin—"this one is bad; that one is worse." Anything contrary to God's law is sin, and the temptation to rationalize it is strong. Resist condemning your friend for her sin of gluttony. Also, remember that if you continue to smoke, you are admonished not to indulge in a practice that may not bother you when you are with someone whom it does bother.

Instead, examine your life before God and follow His

leading as to how you should live. Concentrate on what God is saying to you, and leave the teaching on individual standards in her life to the prompting of the Holy Spirit and the truth of the Scriptures.

❧ *For God will bring every act to judgment, everything which is hidden, whether it is good or evil. (Ecclesiastes 12:14)*
❧ *Or do you not know that your body is a temple of the Holy Spirit who is in you, whom you have from God, and that you are not your own? (1 Corinthians 6:19)*

~

4. My husband recently infected me with a sexually transmitted disease he got from a one-night fling with a coworker. I am very angry at God for allowing this to happen when I've been a committed Christian for years. How can I find resolution?

*M*y heart goes out to you and the anguish you are experiencing. All disease, including STDs, are a result of the sinful world in which we live. When Adam chose to sin, he unleashed all evil, and disease is one of the dreadful consequences. I know your actions did not bring about this consequence, but when you married, you and your husband became one flesh. In Corinthians, God explains that what happens to one part of the body affects the entire body. You are seeing this truth in your life right now. Because your husband sinned, you share in the consequence of that because you are a part of your husband.

The anger you are experiencing is understandable. Accept the fact that God did not give you the disease. Neither is He shocked or angry by your rage. You need to openly express to God everything you are feeling and then ask Him to help you find good in it. Journaling is an excellent way of dealing with extreme emotions. Hebrews says, "Let us therefore draw near with confidence to the throne of grace, that we may receive mercy and may find grace to help in time of need" (4:16). After you have vented all the tangled feelings within you, sit quietly and let God speak to you. You will learn that God is still close and is still working on you. He loves you very much. God does use suffering to bring about good changes in our lives. Some of his reasons for allowing suffering are to strengthen our faith or to judge sin. So in your prayers, pray for your husband, that he will be convicted of his sin and turn away from it.

Finally, you asked how you could find resolution. You will find peace when you forgive your husband. In Mark, chapter 11, verse 25, God instructs us, "Whenever you stand praying, forgive, if you have anything against anyone, so that your Father who is in Heaven will also forgive you your transgressions." It does not list who is worthy to be forgiven, it says "anything against anyone," indicating that the forgiveness is not conditional. This is because in order for someone who has been wronged to be healed, they must forgive the one who harmed them. When you release them by forgiving them, you will begin to be healed from your anger.

ꙮ *Answer me, O LORD, for Your loving kindness is good; according to the greatness of Your compassion, turn to me. (Psalms 69:16)*
ꙮ *Therefore let us draw near with confidence to the throne of grace, so that we may receive mercy and find grace to help in time of need. (Hebrew 4:16)*

⌒

5. I am opposed to teenage sexual activity. Recently though, I discovered that my oldest daughter (age sixteen) and her boyfriend have been sexually active for several months.

Don't I have a responsibility to protect her health by giving her birth control?

*A*s reasonable as your conclusion sounds, you are assuming that pregnancy is the only negative result of premarital sex. But consider this:

- Sex outside of marriage is against God's law (I Thessalonians 4:3–5). All sin hinders our relationship with God and harms us spiritually.
- You say you are against their sexual activity, so what does providing her with birth control tell her now?
- By providing birth control, you are buying into the myth that once teens begin having sex, they will not stop. Why not? Have you asked her why she is having sex? Does she know she can say *no* even now?
- STDs are deadly. The Center for Disease Control's latest statistic estimates that chlamydia infects 3 to 5 million people every year. The HIV virus can easily pass through the weave of a condom. Syphilis can go undetected for years with crippling effects on her health or any children she may plan to have.
- By providing birth control for your oldest child's sexual activity, what message are you giving her siblings?

Dealing with a teen's premarital sex cannot be done by canned philosophies. You need to engage the help of her youth leader, her physician, and anyone else with influence in her life to get across the message that you oppose her activity and will continue to do so until she stops such destructive behavior. You do not mention her father; he too can be a great deterrent. He needs to speak to her young man. In direct contrast to more liberal thinkers, I believe there's too much ennui on this subject from parents and not enough outspoken, clearly stated reasons why you disapprove. I hope I've given you some food for thought.

∾ *For I, the LORD, do not change; therefore you, O sons of Jacob, are not consumed. (Malachi 3:6)*

∾ *Flee immorality. Every other sin that a man commits is outside the body, but the immoral man sins against his own body. (1 Corinthians 6:18)*

∼

6. I have been experiencing severe headaches. The doctor has suggested they may be triggered by post-traumatic stress syndrome. Why does the medical profession insist on "deeper" meanings to a physical ailment? All I need is some good medicine.

Your doctor understands that our emotional state is intrinsically connected to our physical condition. His undoubtedly superior medical knowledge has discerned something in your symptoms that leads him to believe that you have experienced emotional trauma at some time. He knows that just medicating the physical symptoms will not heal the source of your pain. If you experienced abuse in your past and have not been able to deal with it in a way that has brought resolution into your life, then you could be suffering from post-traumatic stress syndrome. It is a very real medical condition. The pain from whatever happened to you cannot be dealt with by stuffing it away and vowing never to think about it again. I cannot give you specific direction to lay the demons from your past to rest. I can tell you that freedom from bondage is one of the perks of serving Jesus Christ. Jesus can make good on His promise to bind up the heartbroken, liberate those in captivity, and release those held in prisons (Isaiah 61:1). He can help you pull the painful images from your emotional closet, and begin to sort them and lay them to rest. Ignoring problems does not make them any less problematic in our lives. They must be dealt with.

There are many good self-help books that give you positive steps to take, but you probably will do best by seeking out a Christian counselor. One of the gifts of the Holy Spirit in 1 Corinthians, chapter 12, is the gift of edification. Edifying can be defined as practically applying God's truth in your life. A Christian counselor will be instrumental in melding Scripture with application to bring healing in your life. Therefore, when you call for an appointment, ask the counselor if she uses the Bible as the foundation for her counseling. If she does not, thank her and keep looking. Your pastor may know someone dependable to recommend.

I do know, from personal experience, that keeping a journal is a very cleansing experience. Interestingly, our hands sometimes can communicate hidden thoughts that our conscious minds and voices will not. Look in the bibliography for some resources and speak to your pastor for direction.

⇗ *Bright eyes gladden the heart; good news puts fat on the bones. (Proverbs 15:30)*
⇗ *A joyful heart is good medicine, but a broken spirit dries up the bones. (Proverbs 17:22)*

7. I know a good Christian wouldn't suffer from depression, but when it happens, are there spiritual steps I should take? And is taking antidepressants wrong?

Depression is a normal emotional response. Our bodies are not equipped to remain on an extended "high"; and when we have experienced one, the common reaction will be depression. Depression that lasts several days is normal and nothing to be concerned about. Depression becomes a problem when it is prolonged, lasting weeks and even into months.

The really great thing about the Bible is it displays people as they really are. Nowhere in Scripture do you find God disguising people's real selves. Therefore, you need to know that there are people in the Bible who suffered from depression. The Prophet Elijah was one and King Saul was another. Depression is not an easy one-fits-all diagnosis. If someone has a chemical imbalance, such as not producing enough serotonin, I guarantee you they will battle depression whether they are Christians or not.

Guilt is a common symptom of depression. Do not pile more guilt on yourself by insisting that you've failed God with your lack of faith.

The really great thing about being a Christian is that first of all we can pray for and believe that God will heal us of the imbalance. Second, we can have peace that if we are not healed (or until we are) He will walk through these valley times with us. As a lifelong sufferer of depression discovered, "I can survive by hugging the Lord tighter."

Also try to implement these practical steps when you first feel depression creeping in on you:

- Start being thankful for what you have.
- Forgive yourself.
- Try to get out of the house every day.
- Get enough sleep.
- Adjust grooming habits so they are as easy as possible. Shower and dress every day.
- Don't lay a guilt trip on yourself if you need an anti-depressant.
- Don't be hard on yourself. Love yourself, because God does!
- Don't dwell on the "shoulds" of life—I "should do this, I should do that . . ."

- Stay away from "toxic" people—you have enough to handle right now without taking grief from them.
- Pray many times every day and read short portions of Scripture.
- Reach out and touch family and friends, even if just on the phone.
- Ask those whom you can trust to pray for you. Prayer really works.

Regarding taking antidepressants, God does not condemn us for using medication. Satan would like to place extra burdens on you by telling you that you are letting God down. But God does not accuse us in this manner. Especially if your depression is a result of a chemical problem, you will need medicine to correct the deficiency.

While you take medication, *do not* decide on your own to stop taking the medication. Tragic consequences can occur from stopping these types of medications cold turkey. God will make it abundantly clear to you and your doctors when the time comes that you no longer need medication. More than anything, accept the help that is available and get yourself well.

∽ *Now the Spirit of the LORD departed from Saul, and an evil spirit from the LORD terrorized him. (1 Samuel 16:14)*
∽ *Blessed are those who mourn, for they shall be comforted. (Matthew 5:4)*

8. Our five-year-old is a diabetic. It's not just birthday parties that are a problem, it is its effect on his whole life. What can I do to help him?

*B*eing married to a man with diabetes, I am aware that the dietary rules for diabetics have changed drastically over the years. Depending on the severity of your child's condition, and by talking with the doctor about this problem, you may be able to allow him small amounts of celebratory foods once in a while. If he is severely diabetic, he will have to deal with these restrictions all his life and your attitude will be instrumental in accepting it. I'd go to great lengths to provide treats for him to eat at any social situation because if other mothers know that you will give that help, he will not be excluded from social activities.

I detect from your question that you are overwhelmed with sadness over your child's disease. God offers hope to all of us for any situation in life. Diabetes is no harder for God to heal than the common cold, and I would encourage you to read Scripture that demonstrate His healing power over any disease. Your best help will be to understand that your son will reflect your attitude and it in turn will affect his ability to cope with the day-to-day limitations. Remember that in our weakness God's power is made strong (2 Corinthians 12:19), and that God can bring good out of any situation if we allow Him to work (Romans 8:28).

Do not dwell on his limitations or allow him to center on them, but rather direct his outlook to what he is able to do. Encourage his creativity and seek to expand yours to find ways to make his life more fulfilling. You want to teach him self-acceptance and to look outward. Talk often about the hope of healing and remember to pray every day for him to be healed.

∾ *The chastening for our well-being fell upon Him, and by His scourging we are healed. (Isaiah 53:5)*
∾ *And He healed many who were ill with various diseases. (Mark 1:34)*

9. My children react negatively to sugars, yet they get cookies and sweet juice every week in Sunday school. I feel that the teacher has a responsibility to respect my wishes, but she refuses to change her ways. What should be my next step?

There appears to be a relational problem between you and the teacher. Problems within a local body were the impetus for most of Paul's letters to the various churches. There were the ladies, Euodia and Syntyche, whose fighting brought unrest to the church in Philippi, and Onesimus, the slave who ran away. So this personal conflict is not just a little difference of opinion, it is something that can affect your entire local body. Since you indicate that you have spoken to her regarding it and there has been no change, you have two choices: You can drop the whole situation or you can pursue it. I encourage you to be forgiving and not make it a point of any further contention. Instead, take the responsibility to provide healthier snacks for the entire class. This will allay your fears regarding your children eating junk food without placing an additional burden on their teacher.

In the teacher's defense, the type of snacks she provides is probably more readily accepted by the students than a healthier choice would be. I imagine her aim is to "reward" them, in which case that would motivate her choice.

∞ *What is desirable in a man is his kindness. (Proverbs 19:22)*
∞ *Be devoted to one another in brotherly love; give preference to one another in honor. (Romans 12:10)*

⌒

10. Friends of ours have a child who's been recently diagnosed with Tourette's syndrome. He is only eight years old but sometimes right in church he yells out a swear word, or

he will reach over and pinch a woman's breast. I am very confused. I know Tourette's is a disease, but it seems to me that a Christian child would not be yelling out obscenities or doing inappropriate touching. I am beginning to wonder if he isn't demon possessed. Am I misjudging?

*M*y husband and I were in a pastoral support group for many years, and one of the couples faced exactly what you described. Their middle son was seven years old when he was diagnosed with Tourette's syndrome. We prayed and cried with them as they dealt with their pain and bewilderment over this disease.

I certainly will never say that behavior such as you described cannot be the result of demonic possession. However, I believe that Tourette's syndrome is truly a disease of the nervous system. As such, it does not have anything more to do with demonic activity than any other disease, all of which are a result of sin entering the world through Adam. It is a sad and burdensome part of our world.

The symptoms you described are called *coprolalia* and make me believe your friend's son has an unusually severe case. Because of his age, he probably has not yet had the time or training to learn some coping skills. As time and maturity come upon him, you will probably find that he will learn to mask his overt symptoms more effectively.

But more important, I do hope your church and community will rally around this family. They need protection from thoughtless remarks; they need support for the burden this places on their home; and they need relief. If you are able, offer to baby-sit on a regular basis to allow the parents time to emotionally recharge. The constant care of a person with any disability is very emotionally draining. If baby-sitting is not an option, seek other ways to help, such as supplying an evening meal on a regular basis.

❧ *He has not ignored the suffering of the needy. He has not turned and walked away. He has listened to their cries for help. (Psalms 22:24 NLT)*

෴ *For when your faith is tested, your endurance has a chance to grow. (James 1:3 NLT)*

~

11. Most conservative Christians believe that drinking alcohol is sinful, but how do they explain "a little wine is good for the stomach" (1 Timothy 5:23)?

This verse is best looked at in the light of the culture and time in which it was written. It is more likely an encouragement from the Apostle Paul to his protégé, Timothy, to care for his health. Historical references seem to indicate that Timothy had a less-than-robust nature; and in this passage, Paul is warning him regarding the stress and strains that accompany the ministry. He was encouraging him to accept medicinal help in surviving the ministry. During biblical times, while there were natural medicines, there wasn't the vast array of antibiotics and medications that are available today. While many natural herbs were effective in treating some disorders, it seems that all that could be offered for many others was the panacea of alcohol. It served as a disinfectant and numbing aid. The phrase "for the stomach's sake" indicates that it was for medicinal purposes not pleasure. Wine, due to its aging process, aids digestion.

෴ *Then Eli said to her, "How long will you make yourself drunk? Put away your wine from you." (1 Samuel 1:14)*
෴ *No longer drink water exclusively, but use a little wine for the sake of your stomach and your frequent ailments. (1 Timothy 5:23)*

12. Our beautiful fifteen-year-old daughter has an eating disorder. We are at our wits' end; the more we talk and argue about it with her, the worse it becomes. Counseling does not seem to be doing any good. What can we do?

*T*he Web site *www.christiananswers.net* reports that an estimated one-tenth of all women experience an eating disorder at some time in their life. It is an insidious disease among young women in our society.

You need to understand that bingeing, self-induced vomiting, and starvation are forms of self-abuse and demonstrate a hatred of whom God created you to be. You daughter is acting out in her food habits, the turmoil, fear, insecurity, or rage that is lodged within her. If, as you say, counseling hasn't helped, it is not because she hasn't heard the truth, but that she is either willfully or unconsciously refusing to accept the truth.

That being the case, I would, for a time, quit speaking truth about the situation and concentrate on encouragement and love. When communication is difficult, using hugs to bridge the gap is good. Continue to bombard Heaven with your prayers for God to remove the blinders from her heart and eyes.

Also pray for openness for yourself. If she should feel safe enough to verbalize what she is feeling, it may resound unfavorably on you and your husband. Be open to listening without judging. At the root of her problem is a lot of pain and you need to be willing to address its source when revealed.

As a side note: Analyze your attitude toward weight and appearance, as you may be an unsuspecting source of her unrealistic drive for physical perfection.

∾ *My soul, wait silently for God alone, for my expectation is from Him. He only is my rock and my salvation; He is my defense; I shall not be moved. In God is my salvation and my glory; The rock of my strength, and my refuge, is in God. Trust in Him at all times, you people; pour out your heart before Him; God is a refuge to us. (Psalm 62:5–8 NKJV)*

∾ *We do not have a High Priest who cannot sympathize with our weaknesses . . . (Hebrews 4:15 NKJV)*

∼

13. My mother recently died after a three-year battle with cancer. I am now finding myself consumed with the fear that I have cancer. I keep finding symptoms in my body; I cannot sleep; I am having trouble letting my kids out of my sight for fear I will not live to see their return. Can you help me or do I need a shrink?

Keep track of what triggers your fear and fight it with the perfect weapon: God's Word. Praise God out loud when fear overwhelms you, praise Him for life, praise Him for protection for your children. Christians have a weapon no one else has—the ability to transform their mind through God's Word. Whenever thoughts that are contrary to God's Word come into your mind, immediately force them out with God's Word. Speak out loud something like, "In the name of Jesus, I command this fear to be gone." Then (because nature abhors a vacuum) replace that wrong thinking with a biblical truth: "God has not given me a spirit of fear but one of a sound mind and thought" (1 Timothy 1:7), or some other verse that speaks to your specific situation. Every time you recognize your self-talk is leading you into negativism and despair, immediately break the cycle with God's Word.

Seek out a support group in your community and begin attending. During the meetings you will discover that much of what you are experiencing is normal and shared by many others there. They will offer hope and encouragement for you.

∾ *"For I know the plans that I have for you," declares the LORD, "plans for welfare and not for calamity to give you a future and a hope." (Jeremiah 29:11)*

∾ *Rejoice with those who rejoice, and weep with those who weep. (Romans 12:15)*

~

14. Recently a friend in our Bible study was diagnosed with cancer, and the doctors give her six months to live. I hate myself because I haven't called or spoken to her, but I just do not know what to say. Is it too late for me to make amends?

I do not think it is too late at all; and I imagine you'll find her very understanding, but do it now. All you need to say is the truth: "I am so sorry for my absence. I just didn't know what to say. But I hope you'll forgive me, because I've never stopped loving you and being concerned about it." A hug says more than anything else will.

Offer her practical help such as doing her weekly shopping. Ask if you can come vacuum her house once a week. If her kids are the same age as yours, invite them over regularly so they'll have a safe link to relate to when their mom does pass away.

After you've asked for forgiveness, forgive yourself. Let loose regrets and focus on her needs. Just make sure that in your newfound enthusiasm to help, you don't go faster than she is ready for. In other words, allow her to keep to her regular schedule to the extent that she is able and cares to. The time will come, and soon, that she will need to lean on all of her friends.

Above all, do not give up praying for her healing, praying for her, praying for the family.

∾ *I went about as though it were my friend or brother; I bowed down mourning, as one who sorrows for a mother. (Psalms 35:14)*

∾ *Weep with those who weep. (Romans 12:15)*

∾

15. Wouldn't I be a better Christian if I followed the strict dietary laws laid out in the Old Testament?

*N*o, it is not true that you will be a better Christian by following the Law. In fact, deliverance from the restrictions of the Law was the intent of Christ's coming. He said He came to set us free. In strictly observing any sets of rules, we are attempting to make ourselves more acceptable to God. Nothing we can do can make God love us any more or any less than He already does. His love is already full, complete, and total.

It is true you may be a healthier individual if you followed stricter dietary laws. Our freedom is not to be a license for excess. Overeating is a serious problem among today's generation. So it is not wrong to follow a strict diet out of a desire to be healthier. It is simply that it does not in itself give you any spiritual advantage in your relationship with Jesus, which comes when we accept Him in our lives. He did everything necessary to make us complete and whole Christians by his death and Resurrection.

∾ *He has sent me to bind up the brokenhearted, To proclaim liberty to captives And freedom to prisoners. (Isaiah 61:1)*

∾ *It was for freedom that Christ set us free; therefore keep standing firm and do not be subject again to a yoke of slavery. (Galatians 5:1)*

171

16. I exercise regularly and would never consider getting fat. I feel this is showing respect to God, but my husband has hinted that he feels I am vain.

*I*f you exercise in order to keep your body healthy, then you are doing it for the right motives. It is a habit that will reap you rewards in better health than a sedentary life would give you.

Perhaps he feels that you spend an inordinate amount of time pursuing health. How much time a day/week do you exercise? Do you make a big thing out of it or simply do it? Do you spend more time exercising your body than you do exercising spiritually?

The most obvious way to find out what he is thinking is simply to ask him if he is concerned about how much you exercise and why that is.

∾ *She girds herself with strength And makes her arms strong. (Proverbs 31:17)*
∾ *For bodily discipline is only of little profit, but godliness is profitable for all things, since it holds promise for the present life and also for the life to come. (1 Timothy 4:8)*

∾

17. All of my life I have hated my appearance because of the large nose I inherited from my father. Now that I am financially able to afford cosmetic surgery, would it be wrong to choose it?

*T*here isn't anything sinful about having cosmetic surgery. If you are able to afford it—you are not taking the grocery money to finance it—then I say go for it. I know there are those who will hint to you that it is a selfish use of money. They may even say that you should give that money to feed the poor. However, you can discount their reasoning as illogical, because people pay large amounts of money for nonessentials all the time. Our comfortable cars are a good example. Couldn't we go by bus just as well? When God blesses us, He does not wish for it to create guilt and anguish in our life.

However, before you choose to have surgery, you need to examine the reasons you wish to change your nose. Make sure that the expense and pain of getting a new nose will be worth it. Using cosmetics to make us feel better about ourselves is fine only if we can still like ourselves without them. Otherwise, when you get your nose done, you may then notice some other feature of your body that is not to your liking and want to alter it. As you can see, this could continue until you have a totally new body, and in the end you might still be dissatisfied with your appearance.

❧ *Now when the turn of each young lady came to go in to King Ahasuerus, after the end of her twelve months under the regulations for the women—for the days of their beautification were completed as follows: six months with oil of myrrh and six months with spices and the cosmetics for women. (Esther 2:12)*

❧ *Your adornment must not be merely external—braiding the hair, and wearing gold jewelry, or putting on dresses; but let it be the hidden person of the heart, with the imperishable quality of a gentle and quiet spirit, which is precious in the sight of God. (1 Peter 3:3–4)*

❧

18. Everything we eat seems to eventually be found out to lead to cancer. Is there any diet that we know will be safe for us?

I've always believed we are so much better off if we observe moderation in our diets rather than follow any excessive health fad. As a matter of fact, following all the latest findings can be frustrating. They seem to eventually cancel themselves out somewhere down the line. Listen to your doctor and eat in moderation and trust God to keep you healthy. Keep your diet in perspective: God has your days planned and the number of your days as well. What we can do is improve the quality of our life by good habits to keep us healthier.

∾ *For by me your days will be multiplied, and years of life will be added to you. (Proverbs 9:11)*
∾ *And which of you by worrying can add a single hour to his life's span? (Luke 12:25)*

∼

19. I've been a smoker for almost twenty years. I recently felt that God would be pleased by me stopping, but it has brought me nothing but frustration, weight gain, and depression. Could I have been mistaken?

*N*o. Many worthwhile goals are difficult and require discipline. We do not act on feelings alone when trying to follow God. The Holy Spirit has spoken to your spirit, urging you to give up an unhealthy habit. What you are attempting is obedience and whenever we are obedient to God; our adversary, Satan, comes in with everything at his disposal to keep us from taking this step and growing spiritually. Discouragement is one of the most effective weapons in Satan's arsenal. So do not depend on your feelings during this time. We are to glorify God with our lives and our bodies. The evidence on the harm of smoking is too overwhelming to just brush off. New habits are very hard to establish. It takes discipline, support, and the help of the Holy Spirit to complete His work in our lives. Do not give up. You will be very glad you persevered.

∾ *He who neglects discipline despises himself, but he who listens to reproof acquires understanding. (Proverbs 15:32)*
∾ *All discipline for the moment seems not to be joyful, but sorrowful; yet to those who have been trained by it, afterwards it yields the peaceful fruit of righteousness. (Hebrews 12:11)*

∼

20. It's been well documented that Americans overeat. So why is it that whenever Christians get together we insist on having food?

No doubt habit and tradition play a big part in it. For example, what's Thanksgiving if we do not eat turkey? But one reason I believe is that God always linked food and celebrations. God loves fellowshipping with His people. He instituted many festivals that He wanted His people to observe each year. And each one had special food that was a part of the celebration. So if God put together merrymaking, traditions, and food, why would we change it?

If you are concerned about overeating, which indeed is a serious problem in affluent nations, then use your ingenuity to provide healthful, low-fat, low-cholesterol foods when you entertain.

An additional note on how God views food is to realize that there will be food in Heaven. In Revelation, God describes a future banquet He will give to all Saints that will last for seven years. It may seem odd since we will not need to eat food to survive in Heaven, but there seems to be an integral link in God's eyes between celebration and food. Therefore, I no longer feel apologetic in always having food.

I am simply following God's example.

> *They asked, and He brought quail, and satisfied them with the bread of heaven. (Psalms 105:40)*
> *Then he said to me, "Write, 'Blessed are those who are invited to the marriage supper of the Lamb.'" And he said to me, "These are true words of God." (Revelation 19:9)*

~

21. When my child gets sick and the first thing I do is call the doctor, does that mean I do not believe God can heal my child?

I do not think your problem is unbelief in God's ability to heal your child. It may be that you have a problem believing that He *will* heal your child. There is a subtle but profound difference. The fact that you call the doctor is wise. God has blessed us with modern medicine and it is available for our use; so, you need to take advantage of what is available to you.

Concurrently though, you need to exercise your faith in what God will do on your behalf. He is waiting to meet your need. When our children are sick, we need to pray for their healing and believe that they will be healed. In James, we also are instructed to call for the elders in our church to come and pray. The support of our Christian family is very encouraging in difficult times. Whether the healing occurs as a result of modern medicine or in an instant through the healing touch of Jesus is immaterial, for ultimately it all comes from Him.

> *For I, the LORD, am your healer. (Exodus 15:26)*
> *Jesus was going through all the cities and villages, teaching in their synagogues and proclaiming the gospel of the kingdom, and healing every kind of disease and every kind of sickness. (Matthew 9:35)*

22. I am attracted to holistic medicine. Can it be a godly approach to health and healing?

"*H*olistic" is really too general of a term to be able to make a judgment on whether the practices you are considering are harmless or not. Any medicine that relates to the whole body is not, in itself, wrong. But words can be deceiving and some medical practices that call themselves holistic can in fact be masquerading as alternative medicines, which incorporate New Age practices into their treatment. Don't rely on terms, but look for warning signs such as crystals, channeling, or horoscopes in the diagnosis or treatment. If your holistic practitioner employs any of these methods, I would stress that you not become involved with them. Anything that involves the occult, whether it admits it or not, is to be shunned by Christians.

On the other hand, a homeopathic approach to medicine, stressing a scientific base but using natural herbs and incorporating a healthy diet and exercise, would be an alternative you may want to look in to and try. Anytime we find a natural way to treat out bodies that works, it is much healthier than employing drugs that can remain in our system far longer than is healthy and have unwanted side effects.

༄ *"For I will restore you to health and I will heal you of your wounds," declares the Lord. (Jeremiah 30:17)*
༄ *On either side of the river was the tree of life, bearing twelve kinds of fruit, yielding its fruit every month; and the leaves of the tree were for the healing of the nations. (Revelation 22:2)*

CAREER AND THE WORKPLACE

1. How do I reconcile Christ's teaching of "putting others first" and "thinking of others more highly than ourselves" with the marketplace philosophy of "sell yourself"? Isn't this a self-serving, even haughty attitude?

*I*t is true that God condemns proud and boastful talk. Therefore, hoarding the credit for work done by you and your coworkers or letting people believe you are accomplished in areas in which you have no experience is arrogant and foolhardy. Even if people who do this seem to prosper, remember that the prevailing workplace philosophy may be inconsistent with God's viewpoint. We do not need to "sell" ourselves; we need to be diligent, faithful employees and let our work speak for itself. Much of what is wrong in the workplace is a direct result of inept employees who spend their time self-promoting and inflating their accomplishments in order to get ahead, instead of being diligent workers.

However, neither should we hide our lights under a bushel. When an opportunity presents itself for which we are qualified, we should step forward, always remembering that God knows our lives and us and be willing to let Him open and close the doors. There are many instances in the Bible of God's putting His people in positions of authority. Consider Joseph who was placed second-in-command over all of Egypt. The key principle to keep in mind is that we exhibit integrity in our work and in how we report what work we have done.

∾ *The steps of a righteous [wo]man are established by the Lord. (Psalms 37:23)*
∾ *"Who then is the faithful and wise servant, whom the master has put in charge of the servants in his household to give them their food at the proper time? It will be good for that servant whose master finds him doing so when he returns. I tell you the truth, he will put him in charge of all his possessions." (Matthew 24:45–47 NIV)*

180

2. How do I deal with gossip in the workplace?

*I*n order to avoid being caught in the trap of gossiping, you must realize how much damage it does. Ask God to reveal to your heart just how He views it. When you understand the damage that talking about coworkers does—maligning their character and eroding their self-esteem, their sense of worth—you will have a better reason to avoid it. Your best response is to focus on your work when others begin talking (head down, disinterested attitude), and they will quickly get the message that you are not going to participate.

If, on the other hand, this is becoming a serious problem in your workplace, you could speak out against it. Gossip is like a tenacious weed; once it gets a start, it is very hard to stop, and it grows and grows. Sometimes the only way to deal with it is to attack it head-on and express how hurtful you feel it is to the morale in your workplace.

Finally, make it your own personal campaign to speak words of life to others. Seek ways to encourage, compliment, and uplift your office mates.

❧ *The mouth of the righteous flows with wisdom, but the perverted tongue will be cut out. (Proverbs 10:31)*
❧ *So also the tongue is a small part of the body, and yet it boasts of great things. See how great a forest is set aflame by such a small fire! (James 3:5)*

~

3. My coworkers frequently go out to lunch together and "extend" the lunch hour. What should I do?

*T*he Bible warns us to take care not to defraud another person. If we are collecting eight hours of pay but only working seven hours because we overstay our lunch hour or breaks, we are robbing our employer.

If I am reading your question correctly, your concern isn't that they are taking a longer lunch hour, but that they do not make up the lost time by staying later. If this is a common practice when you are out with them, do not stop going. Just provide your own transportation if the location is not in the building where you work. When your allotted time is up, leave and return to work. If your coworkers are extending their lunch hour when you are not along, leave it to your manager to deal with it as he or she thinks is appropriate.

You yourself seem to understand that extending the lunch hour is as true a case of stealing from your employee as if you took pens and pencils from the workplace.

For the ways of a man are before the eyes of the LORD, and He watches all his paths. (Proverbs 5:21)

Bondservants, be obedient to those who are your masters according to the flesh, with fear and trembling, in sincerity of heart, as to Christ; not with eye service, as men-pleasers, but as bondservants of Christ, doing the will of God from the heart. (Ephesians 6:5–6 NKJV)

4. How can I share my faith effectively at work?

You might be the only Bible your coworkers will read, and your daily life will be the best witness. Emulate Christ's response to the people around Him and look for needs you can meet. Is a coworker caring for an aging or sick relative? Prepare a meal in disposable containers (it is easier for them not to return your dishes) and take it to them at work. Keep postcards in your desk on which to jot an encouraging note and leave on a neighbor's desk.

Remember, nothing will ruin your witness more than preaching instead of working. Focus on being a model employee and let your work speak for your faith. God will provide opportunities on breaks, lunches, and in casual conversation to speak about why you believe as you do, and why your response toward situations may be different from others at work.

∾ *She opens her mouth in wisdom, and the teaching of kindness is on her tongue. (Proverbs 31:26)*
∾ *Let your light shine before men in such a way that they may see your good works, and glorify your Father who is in heaven. (Matthew 5:16)*

~

5. A coworker is spreading untrue stories about my character. How should I handle this?

Jesus seemed to spend most of his earthly ministry being the target of rumors. He was called a drunkard, demon-possessed, and accused of plotting to overthrow the government. In each case, He did not defend Himself. He had His eyes on the goal of fulfilling His Father's mission, and would not be sidetracked by malicious talk.

The Bible demonstrates again and again that truth always wins. The evidence of your character through your work and kindness—even to those who lie about you—will speak more effectively in your defense than verbal rebuttals.

∾ *He will bring forth your righteousness as the light and your judgment as the noonday. (Psalms 37:6)*
∾ *Conduct yourselves with wisdom toward outsiders, making the most of the opportunity. Let your speech always be with grace, as though seasoned with salt, so that you will know how you should respond to each person. (Colossians 4:5–6)*

6. Four of us carpool, and one woman is always late. She has never been so tardy that we've been late to work, but I always feel rushed and upset when I do not arrive ten minutes early to organize my day. Am I wrong to give her an ultimatum?

*Y*our frustration reminds me of Jesus' friend Martha. Her focus, too, was on the amount of work to be done. When she complained to Jesus about Mary's inability to help carry the load, His compassionate response was, "Martha, Martha, you are worried and bothered about so many things, but only a few things are necessary" (Luke 10:39–40). He was pointing out that it was not too much to do that was her root problem, it was wrong priorities.

Have compassion for your friend. Ask if there's something you can do to help her. Maybe she needs a friendly wake-up call. You can also relieve anxiety by planning ahead. Since you know you'll be walking through the door of your office at 8:00 A.M. instead of 7:45, use the last fifteen minutes of your workday to organize for the next morning.

Always, honesty is the best option. Share with her how you feel about running so close to the time clock. Maybe she isn't aware of how hard it is on you. Finally, if nothing brings about a compromise, then you should explore other carpool options in your area.

∾ *A friend loves at all times, and a brother is born for adversity. (Proverbs 17:17)*
∾ *Be devoted to one another in brotherly love; give preference to one another in honor. (Romans 12:10)*

~

7. Office celebrations are getting out of hand. Now I am approached weekly for a donation I really cannot afford. Can I just say *no*?

*Y*ou probably aren't the only one strapped financially, but there's something so very drab about complaining about lack of money. We serve a generous God who values the principles of openhandedness. Proverb 22, verse 9, promises that "he who is generous will be blessed." Be happy to contribute to someone else's good fortune. Proverb 16, verse 9, tells us how to do this: "The mind of man plans his way, but the Lord directs his steps." Gift-giving money needs to become a part of your budget. As pastors, my husband and I receive joy in sharing in every congregant's special events. So we have become masters at creative ways to give affordable gifts. Tune in to the creativity God gave you to find a unique gift that does not break your budget. Maybe there is a one-of-a-kind memento you can make such as a personalized wedding album. With a little forethought and planning, you can find ways to celebrate important events in the lives of friends without assaulting your budget.

Now that I've said that, I am aware that sometimes offices do celebrations for every little thing and it isn't a matter of not wishing to be generous but really is a financial burden. If they celebrate because Lisa had her braces removed or if they set the amount of money you should contribute, you will have to speak up and tell them that you have *X* amount of money each month and once it is gone, there isn't any more. If this is common behavior, you can probably also relieve many others by suggesting that a fund be set up to which everyone contributes a small amount each month and out of which all gifts and celebrations are paid for.

❧ *But good people will be generous to others and will be blessed for all they do. (Isaiah 32:8 NLT)*
❧ *Prepare your generous gift beforehand, which you had previously promised, that it may be ready as a matter of generosity and not as a grudging obligation. (2 Corinthians 9:5 NKJV)*

8. I have been very blessed in my job and now have been offered a promotion as regional field manager. It means a move of 500 miles. My husband is refusing to discuss moving, citing our settled life here and the children's contentment with school and friends. Any suggestions?

As hard as this seems now, your first priority is your family. After an open discussion of all the options, you need to accept and honor your husband's decision. In our "me first" "my fulfillment is most important" society, this sounds like career suicide, but that is the beauty of serving God. Since He set up the framework of the family, making the man responsible for the final decision, you can trust God to either change your husband's mind or bless your career in another way. Proverb 21, verse 1, says that God can turn the heart of a king, so He is able to change your husband's heart if that would be best.

I will say, however, that if your husband isn't willing to discuss this opening, you are going to face it again when you are offered another promotion. I sense that there might be more involved here. Perhaps your husband is not comfortable with your success and its implications. You should pursue more discussion on this to get to the bottom of his unwillingness to accept your good fortune. It may be that a mediator such as a Christian counselor could help you take the emotion out of the situation and help you both fully explore the ramifications of staying or moving.

∾ *Delight thyself also in the Lord; and he shall give thee the desires of thine heart. (Psalms 37:4 KJV)*
∾ *Wives, be subject to your own husbands, as to the Lord. For the husband is head of the wife, as Christ also is head of the church, He Himself being the Savior of the body. (Ephesians 5:22–23)*

9. Even though my three kids are reasonably healthy, routine medical appointments are keeping me away from work on a regular basis. Naturally, my manager is starting to complain, even though I make up the lost time. How should I handle this situation?

*D*uring working hours, you have a responsibility to serve your employer to the best of your ability. To facilitate this, ask your husband to help share the load of regular appointments. Also, discuss your options with your manager before it ruins your job opportunities. Maybe this would be a time to discuss the company creating flextime, something many corporations are embracing. You may also have to make the appointments on weekends, as distasteful as that may be. Remember to keep the long view: This is a season of your life. This time of intensive parenting will not intrude forever, so do not let it get you down.

ᔰ *There is an appointed time for everything. And there is a time for every event under heaven. (Ecclesiastes. 3:1)*
ᔰ *No one can serve two masters; for either he will hate the one and love the other, or else he will be loyal to the one and despise the other. (Matthew 6:24 NKJV)*

~

10. A coworker always seems to need a lift to work. I didn't mind at first as it is on my way, but now that it's become an almost weekly occurrence, I am beginning to feel taken advantage of. She has never offered to help with gas. What should I do?

*I*f it is not out of your way, continue to help her out. Do not begrudge a colleague something that does not cost you anything. Put yourself in her shoes and imagine how hard it must be to ask continually for rides to work.

If it is an inconvenience because it is out of your way, or you have to amend your coming and going to accommodate her working schedule, then it would be proper to reply that you do not mind doing it occasionally but since you plan to run errands after work or go directly on to another engagement, you will not be able to provide her transportation on an ongoing basis.

Truthfully, once a week does not seem like too much an inconvenience, unless you get the sense that the number of times she asks is going to increase, which is why you are asking in the first place.

If it becomes more than a weekly occurrence, there is nothing wrong in being up-front and asking her to contribute to the gas bill. Just one additional consideration: Be sure and check with your insurance company regarding your liability when she pays for the gas.

ᴄᴡ *One who is gracious to a poor man lends to the LORD, and He will repay him for his good deed. (Proverbs 19:17)*

ᴄᴡ *And one of you says to them, "Go in peace, be warmed and be filled," and yet you do not give them what is necessary for their body, what use is that? (James 2:16)*

~

11. My kids keep calling me at work. I know my manager does not approve, but I want my kids to know I am available when they need me. What should I do?

Many times when our kids call us, it is for reassurance—the comfort of hearing our voice. Understanding this need for reassurance, begin gently pushing your children to put their faith into action. When you are putting them to bed, memorize Scriptures that speak about God's care.

An important part of our job as parents is transferring our faith to our children and helping them put it into action. It takes patience to help them differentiate between emergencies (when you must be contacted), and simply a desire to touch base with Mom. Children also need a name and number of another adult they can speak with when it is not an emergency.

I sense your children may have too much time alone. Solitude can be very frightening to some children. It may be better to get them into after-school programs or hire an older student to stay with them after school until you get home from work. Just because age-wise you feel they are old enough to be left alone, their maturity level may not be quite up there yet.

☙ *When I am afraid I will put my trust in You. (Psalms 56:3)*
☙ *We learned not to rely on ourselves, but on God. (2 Corinthians 1:9 NLT)*

~

12. There are long down periods at work when there is absolutely nothing to do. My coworkers bring books to read and even knitting. I feel like I am cheating the company even though it is apparent that management does not mind. What do you think?

It does not sound as if the company feels you are doing anything wrong. But idle time is hard for diligent workers. Remember Christ's teaching about heart service and go the extra mile. He reminded us that just doing what's required is the same as what the heathen does, and we need to show the difference Christ makes by exceeding expectations. Ask your manager for books to read to improve your job performance. You can volunteer to work on other projects or help in other departments. Anytime you excel in your job expectations, it will lead to promotion.

But if everything that can be done is taken care of, and your employer has indicated that your presence is needed in case of work to do, but he does not care if you fill in empty time with other activities, use these bonus minutes to pen a letter, write your best-selling novel, or discover the cure for the common cold. My personal feeling is doing something that resembles play, such as knitting or putting together a jigsaw puzzle, is not a professional response to free time from your employer.

∽ *Poor is he who works with a negligent hand, but the hand of the diligent makes rich. (Proverbs 10:4)*
∽ *Let your light so shine before men in such a way that they may see your good works, and glorify your Father who is in heaven. (Matthew 5:16)*

∽

13. My company demands a lot of overtime. The extra money is not enough compensation for the loss of time with my family. This seems to be the norm in corporate America, and I do not think a job change will make it go away. What do you think?

One of the many problems of "keeping ourselves unstained by the world" (James 1:27) is in ordering our priorities and still being viable for today's job market. It is true that many companies, despite what they say, prize loyalty to the company above family commitments. I cannot imagine that this will change, and hiring more employees is discouraged because it hurts a company's bottom line.

You will have to choose whether to keep this job with its requisite overtime or look for another. I would encourage you and your husband to make this a matter of prayer until you receive peace about the choice to take. When we are willing to wait for God's timing, the Father, who loves to give good gifts to His children, will provide the perfect opportunity for you, or move on management to change your company's policy.

If you were originally hired with the understanding that you will work overtime, you need to accept it or look for another position elsewhere. If mandatory overtime is a recent change in policy, you may be able to discuss it and its effect on your family with your manager, and find out if you can work out a compromise or decline it.

Remember, before taking your next job, be sure to discuss overtime expectations at your interview.

∾ *She seeketh wool, and flax, and worketh willingly with her hands. (Proverbs 31:13)*
∾ *Exhort bondservants to be obedient to their own masters, to be well pleasing in all things, not answering back. (Titus 2:9)*

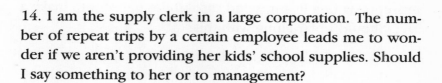

14. I am the supply clerk in a large corporation. The number of repeat trips by a certain employee leads me to wonder if we aren't providing her kids' school supplies. Should I say something to her or to management?

You have to be sure of your facts before accusing someone, but if you know thievery is occurring and do not say anything, it makes you an accessory to the crime. Romans, chapter 13, verse 1, commands us to be in subjection to the governing authorities. If you only suspect that it is occurring, confide your suspicions to your manager, and let her deal with it. If the person is a coworker, you might pose a seemingly innocent question to alert her that you are observing the increased orders: "Irene, I am very concerned about the amount of supplies we are ordering. Do you have any idea why the volume is three times what it was last year?"

Above all, your loyalty lies with your employer. If you do have positive proof that she is cheating the corporation, you are obligated to report it to the proper people within your corporation.

⮞ *A truthful witness saves lives, but he who utters lies is treacherous. (Proverbs 14:25)*

⮞ *Now He was also saying to the disciples, "There was a rich man who had a manager, and this manager was reported to him as squandering his possessions." And he called him and said to him, "What is this I hear about you? Give an accounting of your management, for you can no longer be manager." (Luke 16:1–2)*

~

15. I am a saleswoman for a computer company. Because we're not number one, we're expected to try harder, even to misrepresenting features and capabilities in order to make a sale. Should I play along with this?

*I*t is so easy to let integrity slide. Rationalizing says "it is not a downright lie, so it's not wrong," but God does not see it that way. Deliberately misrepresenting facts is dishonest.

If you are confronted with an order to lie, speak up immediately. Be firm about not speaking anything untruthful. Your employer also needs to remember that asking employees to lie is a crime and cause for them to be reported to the authorities.

⮞ *Let Him weigh me with accurate scales, and let God know my integrity. (Job 31:6)*

⮞ *In all things show yourself to be an example of good deeds, with purity in doctrine, dignified, sound in speech which is beyond reproach, so that the opponent will be put to shame, having nothing bad to say about us. (Titus 2:7–8)*

~

16. I have recently been promoted to a job that will involve quite a bit of traveling with some well-known party types. They have made it clear they are delighted I am going, for since I do not drink I can be their designated driver. I am not happy about baby-sitting a bunch of drunks. Do I have a choice?

This has all the earmarks of a potentially serious situation. I understand your reticence in "baby-sitting" partiers. However if you communicate your real feelings in these terms, you may find yourself ostracized. Your attitude will make for uncomfortable business trips and may adversely affect your opportunities for promotion. Being able to deal with difficult situations gracefully is an important professional skill. In a nonbelligerent manner, tell them that you have made other plans for the evening. When they head out for their evening of fun and take it for granted that you are going to accompany them, just politely excuse yourself, reiterating that you have made different arrangement.

Do it in a smiling, nonjudgmental manner, and after a few more attempts to persuade you, they will understand that you will not be available. If, as it sometimes happens, they are insistent and begin to bait you, answer them honestly about wishing to commit your time to other activities.

~ *Do not let kindness and truth leave you. (Proverbs 3:3)*
~ *Be shrewd as serpents and innocent as doves. (Matthew 10:16)*

17. My husband and I have agreed not to eat alone with a member of the opposite sex. My job requires not only traveling with male colleagues, but business lunches. How do we handle this?

*E*very marriage constantly goes through adjustments. Is there any reason your no-dining-with-opposite-sex rule cannot come up for re-evaluation? When you made it, was there something specific that prompted it? Do you simply believe it is just a wise practice in order to avoid problems?

You need to be aware that with all of the sensitive gender-discrimination issues, in today's business world refusing to dine with a person of the opposite sex can be construed as sexual discrimination because business meals are a legitimate business activity.

Avoiding provocative situations is a wise admonition, but you can observe parameters that make sure the business luncheon remains exactly that. For example:

- You can insist on the meeting taking place in a businesslike setting. In other words, you can decline an invitation to lunch in a hotel room.
- You are not obligated to fraternize after the business is completed.
- Often you can legitimately include a third person to accompany you to help with the presentation.

Only you know how strong your marriage is. It is wise to evaluate what temptations you or your spouse might actually encounter and discuss any areas of concern. Every relationship needs trust between the two partners in order to flourish. If you do not trust each other in situations including the opposite sex, there might be some other problems going on that you are not dealing with.

∾ Encourage the young women to love their husbands, to love their children, to be sensible, pure, workers at home, kind,

being subject to their own husbands, so that the word of God will not be dishonored. (Titus 2:4–5)

∾ *Abstain from all appearance of evil. (1 Thessalonians 5:22 KJV)*

∾

18. I have to work outside the home and yet a number of my friends and family make me feel guilty about leaving my children. How can I defend myself?

The "mommy war" must surely be the longest-running hostility in the civilized world, and it is far from over. There is nothing in the Bible against women having careers. Some well-praised women in the New Testament were Lydia, a prominent businesswoman in her city, and Priscilla, a tentmaker. In the Old Testament, the stories of Ruth, who gleaned fields, Deborah, who led an army, or the energetic woman in Proverb 31, who bought and sold, demonstrate that it was more the norm than otherwise. You do not have to accept others' condemnation.

Maybe, though, your guilt comes because you know your reasons for working are not good ones. If you are working only to bring in extra money, be sure that you are really bringing home anything after the extra costs associated with working have been deducted.

Examine your friends' arguments, discuss your turmoil with your husband, and do what you feel is best for your family. If you do have to work, leave it in God's hands and do not be drawn into an argument with others over a decision you and your husband feel is best. By the way, one perfectly good reason for working is simply because you like it.

∾ *She looks for wool and flax and works with her hands in delight. She is like merchant ships; she brings her food from afar. She rises also while it is still night and gives food to her household and portions to her maidens. She considers a field and buys it; from her earnings she plants a vineyard. (Proverbs 31:13–16)*

~ *Beloved, if our heart does not condemn us, we have confidence before God. (1 John 3:21)*

~

19. Our company just hired a twenty-two-year-old to work alongside me. Because of her age I feel threatened by this. Should I mentor and help her along, even though she may pass me up?

Absolutely! One of the most fulfilling relationships you can enter is to duplicate your strengths in someone else. Deuteronomy tells us that Joshua was "filled with the spirit of wisdom" because of being mentored by Moses (34:9). You will be available for promotion yourself when you have trained someone else to do your job. If I were a young person just starting out, I'd be very grateful to have someone give me a helping hand. The bottom line can be summed up in treating others as you would like to be treated yourself.

~ *Do not withhold good from those to whom it is due, when it is in your power to do it. (Proverbs 3:27)*
~ *Therefore, treat people the same way you want them to treat you. (Matthew 7:12)*

~

20. I am a good baker and like to share my goodies. Would it be misconstrued as bribes if I shower my boss with these treats?

f snacking goes on in your office, and I have not experienced one yet that it does not, just bring enough for everybody. I imagine they will appreciate them very much—until they start gaining weight! Rejoice that God has given you gifts that can bless others.

The only way your generosity could be misconstrued is if you brought treats only to your boss or to others who are in a position of power to give you promotions or other favors in the workplace. So be sure and share with everyone in the office equally and there will not be any misunderstanding.

~ *The generous soul will be made rich. (Proverbs 11:25 NKJV)*
~ *Practice hospitality. (Romans 12:13 NIV)*

~

21. I do job "A." My coworker also does job "A" but makes more money. I feel cheated and taken advantage of. Should I make an issue of this?

*Y*ou do not mention if your coworker had more experience coming into your position or has worked with the company longer. Merit raises and education or training can also come into play. Coveting what another possesses is a violation of the Tenth Commandment.

All being equal, however, it is a federal law that you must receive equal pay for equal work. If you are concerned, you should discuss the situation with your manager. Check that your motives are correct and that you are not just coveting your coworker's paycheck and job.

~ *Do not defraud your neighbor or rob him. Do not hold back the wages of a hired man overnight. (Leviticus 19:13 NIV)*
~ *For the workman deserves his support (his living, his food). (Matthew 10:10 AMP)*

22. In a recent office discussion, I found myself being swayed by my colleagues' opinions and viewpoints. Why do I find it so hard to express another view as clearly?

*W*ords are powerful tools, and often are used to sway opinion in the wrong direction. Take each argument and line it up against the principles found in God's Word. Do your research and see if it agrees with Scripture. Book 2 of Timothy tells us that all Scripture is "profitable for teaching, for reproof, for correction, for training in righteousness; that the man of God [us] may be adequate, equipped" (3:16). Scripture not only gives us the right answers, it equips us to refute ungodly philosophies. Always compare popular thought to the light of the Bible to find if it is genuine truth.

Keep in mind that your purpose in expressing another opinion is not to win a fight but simply to plant a seed in someone's mind. Often people believe something is true simply because they've never heard another view. Be salt and light.

∾ *You are God, and Your words are truth.* (2 Samuel 7:28)
∾ *Always being ready to make a defense to everyone who asks you to give an account for the hope that is in you.* (1 Peter 3:15)

~

23. Political correctness is a much-lauded philosophy in the workplace. But I find many of its tenets to be unbiblical. How can I respect diversity in my coworkers without compromising my faith?

*T*he ostensible aim of the PC-philosophy is to create respect for everyone. This is an honorable goal and makes it easier to adhere to. Christ sat with publicans and sinners, the outcasts of his day, because He saw them through eyes of love. He knew they were created in God's image and therefore worthy of respect. You can treat everyone with respect, including refusing to laugh behind their backs or make derogatory comments. Remembering that it is sin that separates us from God, not [in our eyes] degrees of sin, should help you keep a correct perspective.

The bottom line is that you do not have to agree with another's opinion in order to show respect and regard him or her as a person of value.

∾ *Pleasant words are a honeycomb, sweet to the soul, and healing to the bones. (Proverbs 16:24)*
∾ *Regard one another as more important than yourselves. (Philippians 2:3)*

∼

24. I am in the middle of a sexual harassment lawsuit at work. I am starting to feel like I should drop the charges. What does Scripture say about having mercy and/or justice?

You no doubt know that it probably is not within your ability to stop the lawsuit. Federal laws are very strict about an employer's responsibility to stop harassment in their place of business, and you were correct in reporting it. What you do have control over is your attitude. Keep in mind that your goal should be to create a better work environment for yourself and your coworkers, not to seek revenge for what happened to you.

Christ was the first historical figure who elevated the status of women, and He would never countenance abuse of women. While in the middle of this situation, no doubt your position in the workplace has been made uncomfortable. Be careful that your behavior and reactions cannot be construed as belligerent or provoking by refusing to discuss it with coworkers and treating everyone with respect and consideration. Above all, pray that resolution will come quickly.

    ∾ *You shall do no injustice in judgment; you shall not be partial to the poor nor defer to the great, but you are to judge your neighbor fairly. (Leviticus 19:15)*
    ∾ *Don't repay evil for evil. Don't retaliate when people say unkind things about you. Instead, pay them back with a blessing. (1 Peter 3:8 NLT)*

~

25. I've watched a procession of managers in my Fortune 500 company come in, immediately implement changes that inevitably include personnel layoffs, and then move on to better jobs within two years while we are left to deal with the aftermath of their decisions. What is motivating this destructive behavior?

*G*reed is a powerful motivator, especially in a society that lauds go-getters. I too have watched managers manipulate businesses for the sole purpose of showing greater profits in their quarterly reports. By doing so, it appears they are positive managers and it makes them a better prospect with other companies. In fact, their greed destroys companies as they rape the profits during a few years by implementing business practices that they would not use if they intended to remain with the company and expected it to support them for the rest of their life.

    ∾ *Whoever loves money never has money enough; whoever loves wealth is never satisfied with his income. This too is meaningless. (Ecclesiastes 5:10 NIV)*
    ∾ *The love of money is a root of all sorts of evil. (1 Timothy 6:10)*

26. My husband is miserable in his search for the perfect job. In the last year he has had three jobs, all with very difficult bosses whom he has been unable to please. Can you share the key to him finding the perfect job?

I sense God is trying to get your husband's attention and that your sympathy may be hindering Him. In most circumstances, three jobs in a year denotes a poor servant attitude. It may be that your husband is trying to find a job that will give him a sense of fulfillment, when only God can do that. There is no perfect job, even though there is nothing wrong with seeking a satisfying vocation.

As you can see, I do not know enough about his circumstances, but you need to take your hand off the situation. When he complains, assure him you are praying for him. If he quits, do not be quick to step in and save the family; instead, assure him you know he will find another job quickly because his family is depending on him. I firmly believe that sometimes women step ahead of God when their husbands hit tough times. Your best help will be done in prayer.

༖ *So I decided there is nothing better than to enjoy food and drink and to find satisfaction in work. Then I realized that this pleasure is from the hand of God. For who can eat or enjoy anything apart from him? (Ecclesiastes 2:24–25)*
༖ *Whatever you do, do your work heartily, as for the Lord rather than for men. (Colossians 3:23)*

~

27. My boss is immoral, dishonest, unkind, and basically just a jerk. How can I be expected to respect him?

We submit ourselves to authority because God commands us to honor those in authority over us, not because that person deserves it. In order to give him respect, you need to differentiate between the person and the position. To reject his authority simply because he does not fulfill your moral code is as much an error as it would be for you to disregard a summons to court because you think the lawsuit is frivolous.

Pray for him. Prayer has many benefits. It will shape and mold your attitude toward your boss and also activate the Holy Spirit to work in his life. Prayer will give you the grace to look at him through Christ's eyes and make honoring him so much easier.

~ *If a ruler's anger rises against you, do not leave your post; calmness can lay great errors to rest. (Ecclesiastes 10:4 NIV)*
~ *Obey your leaders and submit to them, for they keep watch over your souls as those who will give an account. (Hebrews 13:17)*

~

28. I've always wanted to have a career in politics. Now that my kids are grown, I am considering running for a local office, but the risk is breathtaking. Should I try it?

This sounds like a very exciting option that has been opened to you. Why do you suppose you are considering this? Maybe God planted a seed in your heart and is directing your life in another direction. I can assure you that politics will be here long after you are gone, so it does not need your decision immediately. Instead, pray about it, do research on how you would go about putting in your name as a candidate, do some volunteering on issues that interest you. Talk to many people whose opinions you value to gain a wider perspective on your feelings. If the only thing that is holding you back is fear, though, that is definitely not something that should influence your decision. Remember all the people in the Bible who began new adventures later in life and be encouraged at what God wants to accomplish in your life now.

∾ *Commit your way to the LORD, Trust also in Him, and He will do it. (Psalms 37:5)*
∾ *For God has not given us a spirit of timidity, but of power and love and discipline. (2 Timothy 1:7)*

~

29. I've been given a project at work that will require an entire life change for me and my family. I am afraid if I do not take the project I will lose my promotion. My family needs the finances, but it will require longer hours than are good for my children and possibly Sunday work. Where in Scripture can I turn for some guidance?

The whole Book gives guidance by the precepts that flow throughout it. God says to love the Lord thy God with all thy mind, heart, spirit, and soul and others as ourselves. So what does that mean? Taking any responsibility that will force us to set aside our relationship with God is wrong, so you have to ask yourself if the job is saying "occasional Sunday work" or "continual Sunday work." But you cannot stop there either, because if so, there would be no medical care on Sundays, and pastors themselves wouldn't work. Following only the letter of the law is legalism. Look at your motivation for wanting the job. Ask yourself what it will do to your family. It may be the best solution for everyone. Consult with your husband exactly what you believe the job is asking of you and ask him how he views it. If you decide to accept it, be open with your children and explain what it entails.

∽ *Where there is no guidance the people fall, but in abundance of counselors there is victory. (Proverbs 11:14)*
∽ *But the worries of the world, and the deceitfulness of riches, and the desires for other things enter in and choke the word, and it becomes unfruitful. (Mark 4:19)*

FINANCES

1. My friend tithes to her church and I know she cannot afford it. Why would she rob her family?

*A*ctually, your friend is hanging on to her one true source of dependable help by honoring God with her tithe. She will be fine because she understands that the obedience is the most important act in Christianity. She knows that she cannot afford not to tithe; for the benefits she reaps far outweigh the monetary value. In actuality we do not own anything; God owns it all and we are merely stewards of what He has given us. She also understands that as hard as it is to make ends meet right now, by tithing she is tapping into God's supernatural supply. God's heart is toward the needy, and it is His pleasure to give us gifts. Ask yourself, "Would I consider robbing my government by not paying taxes? Then why would I consider robbing God by withholding tithes?"

∾ *Will a man rob God? Yet you are robbing Me! But you say, "How have we robbed You? In tithes and offerings. Bring the whole tithe into the storehouse, so that there may be food in My house, and test Me now in this," says the LORD of hosts, "and see if I will not open for you the windows of heaven, and pour out for you a blessing until it overflows." (Malachi 3:8, 10)*
∾ *Give, and it will be given to you. They will pour into your lap a good measure—pressed down, shaken together, and running over. For by your standard of measure it will be measured to you in return. (Luke 6:38)*

~

2. I am confused over what my stand should be regarding gambling. I cannot find anything specifically mentioned in the Bible regarding it, but I'll confess I do like to buy a lottery ticket each week just for the thrill of "what if?" Am I sinning when I do that?

*Y*ou are correct that gambling is not mentioned. The closest we come is the term "casting lots," which was a sort of dice throw used to make decisions. Casting lots did not have monetary value ascribed to it.

Let us just suppose that you do win—what then? The Bible says that money won without work melts away. Extra money does not always solve our financial difficulties. For instance, if you find it difficult to manage your money now, getting a huge infusion of it will not help you manage it any better. The problems that sudden wealth brings are often greater than the benefits. Financial writer Larry Burkett, cites studies that show that fully one-third of the people who win a lottery go bankrupt. Remember, if you want to be happy for a year, win the lottery; if you want to be happy for a lifetime, find something you love to do, and do it the rest of your life.

I agree that setting aside a predetermined amount of your discretionary income to play the lottery isn't wrong, but what example are you setting for your children or friends? It has been shown that gambling can be addictive, and since we are our brother's keeper, people who respect you may be enticed into behavior that you can handle, and find themselves ensnared by it.

~ *Whoever loves money never has money enough; whoever loves wealth is never satisfied with his income. This too is meaningless. (Ecclesiastes 5:10 NIV)*
~ *But the worries of the world, the deceitfulness of riches, and the desires for other things enter in and choke the word, and it becomes unfruitful. (Mark 4:19)*

~

3. As a college student contemplating marriage, I am frustrated at our future with two college loans and two car payments.

Is there any way out of this? How does anybody else do it?

*U*nfortunately, too often everybody else does it by being in debt. We are so conditioned by the world's standards you may be in danger of following the norm, which, in our society means being in debt up to your neck. There are debts that today are almost inevitable—a house payment and a college loan are two whose value usually outweighs the debt. Other possessions you go into debt to acquire just *seem* to be important. We are a possession-laden society. Many things that appear to be a necessity really are not. Even a car is optional if you live in a city that has good public transportation. Clothes, eating out, furniture—these only seem essential until weighed against financial bondage for the rest of your life. If you will honor God in your finances, understand the principle of working toward a future by keeping expenses as low as possible now, you will find that it will work out.

❧ *From your bounty, O God, you provided for the poor. (Psalms 68:10 NIV)*

❧ *Consider the lilies of the field, they toil not nor spin yet Solomon in all his splendor was not clothed like one of these. And why are you worried about clothing? Observe how the lilies of the field grow; they do not toil nor do they spin, yet I say to you that not even Solomon in all his glory clothed himself like one of these. (Matthew 6:28–29)*

~

4. I am facing retirement in less than ten years and fear my income will be inadequate. Is it too late for me to start planning now?

*P*lanning for retirement is certainly a very important consideration for us. However, you need to keep in mind that no one knows the future. You are assuming your income will be inadequate. Truthfully, you do not know what the future holds because you cannot foresee the future. In today's economy, we are seeing many rock-solid investments fall away and many people's portfolios are not producing as they had anticipated.

Therefore, place your trust in the One who said He is from the beginning to the end. He knows what your future holds and what you will need. The first step is to realize that God is your true source. He assures us all through Scripture that if we put Him first in our lives, He will see that all of our needs are taken care of. I have observed firsthand God's provision in the lives of many ministers and other Christians who served God all their life with little financial gain, but God always demonstrates His care for them.

Speaking practically, you need to find an investment counselor who can give practical direction for your situation. He or she will no doubt tell you the first thing you should concentrate on is to pay off all debt, including your mortgage. Together you can devise a plan that will enable you to plan for your later years. Maybe you can relocate to an area of the country that has a lower cost of living. It could be that you will not need to retire fully in ten years but instead go to part-time work.

Do you allow yourself to be conditioned by the world's view of finances? If you give control of them to God, He is a much better market manager than even E. F. Hutton.

∽ *Cast your bread upon the waters, for after many days you will find it again. (Ecclesiastes 11:1 NIV)*
∽ *My God will supply all your needs. (Philippians 4:19)*

5. I am overwhelmed by debt. The cost of keeping a family in today's inflation does not come anywhere near the rise in salary. My wife and I are overwhelmed.

*W*hen we are at our lowest is when God can demonstrate His greatness. There are practical steps you can take, such as seeking credit counseling to help you understand where your money is going and what changes you can make to help your debt; you can repent if you've spent money prodigally; and finally you can ask God for direction for a better job or a second source of income. Above all, remember that with God all things are possible.

You do not say if both of you work. If your wife stays at home, is there something she can do from home that would bring in at least enough to pay for the weekly groceries? Peruse the Help Wanted section of your newspaper and see if anything would be a fit for her. Is she able to work part-time or are you able to work a second part-time job? To people who grew up in the Depression era, our habit of working only a forty-hour week seems spoiled, as they grew up working two and maybe three jobs in order to provide for their families. During a one-year period of our marriage, when we had small children, Mike worked one night a week stocking the local 7-11 store. It paid for a couple tanks of gas for our vehicles during the week.

I want to encourage you by saying that what you really need is hope, and that is what God specializes in. Look to Him; He will never fail you.

∾ Since I am afflicted and needy, let the Lord be mindful of me. You are my help and my deliverer; Do not delay, O my God. (Psalms 40:17)
∾ If you then, being evil, know how to give good gifts to your children, how much more will your Father who is in heaven give what is good to those who ask him? (Matthew 7:11)

6. I would like to be a giving person, yet have almost no financial resources. Do you have any ideas?

Jesus and his disciples had nothing when He decided to give—enough food showed up to feed the masses that turned out to hear Him speak. If you are a willing vessel, God will enable you to be the giver you wish to be. Change your mindset from financial to personal. There are many charitable organizations in your city (no matter how small) and all of them need volunteers. Look one up in the Yellow Pages and offer to give an hour a week or a day a month to work in their organization. Also make sure that what you no longer use is directed to organizations that can put it to good use; old clothing and furniture will bless someone less fortunate. If you look around your neighborhood, you may discover an elderly person who could use your help to mow her lawn once a week, or maybe her failing eyesight keeps her from enjoying the daily paper and you could offer to read part of the paper to her nightly. Ask God to open your eyes to creative possibilities.

∾ *There will always be poor people in the land. Therefore I command you to be openhanded toward your brothers and toward the poor and needy in your land. (Deuteronomy 15:11 NIV)*
∾ *And if you give even a cup of cold water to one of the least of my followers, you will surely be rewarded. (Matthew 10:42 NLT)*

∼

7. We've been invited to be in on the ground floor of a sure-thing money-making deal. How do we know if it is legitimate and if we should invest in it?

You can find out if it is legitimate by asking to see the company charter or by hiring an accountant or attorney to go over the terms. Certainly if it is legitimate there isn't any reason you should not profit from this. However, before making any decision, you need to ask the Lord for direction. Just because something is a sure deal now, does not mean it will remain a good investment. In today's economy anything can happen. But the future is not unknown to God. He will give you peace regarding what your decision should be.

∾ *Where there is no guidance, the people fall, but in abundance of counselors there is victory. (Proverbs 11:14)*
∾ *But if any of you lacks wisdom, let him ask of God, who gives to all generously and without reproach, and it will be given to him. (James 1:5)*

∾

8. **We have a newborn baby girl and my maternity leave is almost up. Because my salary is almost double that of my husband's, we are considering having him stay home to care for the baby while I return to work. Most of our acquaintances think that is a very unscriptural decision. Does the Bible say anything about this?**

As always when making a decision, we need to strip away the rhetoric and boil it down to the basic elements. The fact that you make double the income of your husband is the wrong focus, because who makes the most money is not the only reason on which to base your decision. One element is what do you desire? Do you wish to stay home or are you longing to return to your career? A happy mother is key to a child's emotional environment, and some mothers desire the emotional challenge of a career. If you do wish to stay home, are there are other alternatives you could consider? Can you return to work part-time in the hours that your husband would be home to watch the baby? Can you stay home and work from home (more and more businesses are allowing telecommuting)? Could you open a day care with a couple of children to generate necessary income?

This is a timely question and a one-size-fits-all answer is not available. Providing financially for his family is not the only way a husband demonstrates his role as head of the home. Staying at home to care for your child is certainly an important part of being responsible also. If both of you have discussed it thoroughly and have come to the decision that he is better remaining home and you are better with outside employment, do it. Simply because it does not follow the norm doesn't mean it is wrong. I am not in your shoes, and this may be the best solution for your family. I know that the God we serve understands you and your family intimately, and He can give you peace and direction for this decision.

☙ *Delight yourself in the LORD and he will give you the desires of your heart. (Psalms 37:4)*
☙ *Wives, be subject to your own husbands, as to the Lord. (Ephesians 5:22)*

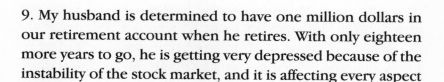

9. My husband is determined to have one million dollars in our retirement account when he retires. With only eighteen more years to go, he is getting very depressed because of the instability of the stock market, and it is affecting every aspect of his life.

*Y*our husband is doomed to disappointment because he is putting his trust in money—the most unstable foundation. Has he considered what could happen even if he manages to meet his goal? Who's to say that inflation will not be so great that one million still won't cover basic living expenses?

His focus is on the wrong thing. Investing and saving are important, but only if done with the understanding that our source is God, not ourselves. In the Book of Luke is a story about a man who had such great wealth he couldn't store it all. He decided to tear down the inadequate barns and build newer, bigger ones to hold all his treasure. And the Scriptures record that God said, "You fool! This very night your soul is required of you." He had totally missed the purpose in living. Depending solely on ourselves is futile and leads to ulcers, heart attacks, and much stress.

꙳ *Some boast in chariots, and some in horses; but we will boast in the name of the LORD our God. (Psalms 20:7)*
꙳ *For where your treasure is, there your heart will be also. (Luke 12:34)*

~

10. I know God tells us to tithe but I cannot afford to do it. Bills are piling up. Will God hate me if I miss a couple months?

I want first of all deal with your fear of God's withholding his love from you. Nothing you can do can make God love you any more or any less. His love toward you is perfect and complete and does not hinge on your performance at all.

Second, in trying to afford your tithe, you are starting at the wrong end, which is trying to figure out God on paper. Many people have experienced the miracle that occurs when we honor God by paying Him first: The remaining 90 percent will go as far or further than the original 100 percent could have. Tithing is the only principle in the Bible for which God offers a guarantee. He tells anyone to try it and just see what blessings He will give that person in return.

I'd encourage you to pray earnestly about this. Ask God for assurance about taking this step. As an example, consider a toddler who is learning to walk. He does not stay on his feet very long at first, but indulgent adults do not get angry at his lack of balance. Instead, they lovingly set him back up on his feet and provide support for his faltering steps until they are firm. In the same way, God is our Heavenly Father, and He does not expect perfection; He will speak to your spirit and give you His assurance that He will walk alongside you as you attempt to follow in obedience.

I guess what I really wish to share with you is that you cannot out-give God. Tithing is one of the greatest blessings you'll ever have. In Malachi, God challenges His people, telling us to test Him by tithing and see what He will do in return for it. When you feel hopeful enough to step out in faith, try it for approximately three to four months. I am confident that you will be amazed when you consider how God has provided for you. Sometimes He provides through monetary blessings, sometimes it is invisible in the protection He places on our health, our vehicles, our belongings—just like the children of Israel who wandered in the desert for forty years without their clothes wearing out, so too will you notice that your vehicles will run better, your health will improve, and many other things that normally have plagued your life will be lessened.

∾ *Honor the LORD from your wealth And from the first of all your produce. (Proverbs 3:9)*
∾ *He who believes in him will not be disappointed. (Romans 9:33)*

∾

11. **All my life I have been taught that having integrity in our financial transactions is very important for Christians. However, due to several unforeseen circumstances, we are**

facing bankruptcy. How can I say I am a Christian when I have cheated those I owe money?

*N*ot all bankruptcy occurs from fiscal irresponsibility. The business world is complex and contains a fragile balance, which often overwhelms people. Certainly losing a job or encountering a serious illness can undermine our financial stability. It is also true, however, that sometimes it occurs because we erred as such by living beyond our means. But our wrongdoing only demonstrates again why we need Christ. The foundational reason Christ came to die for our sins is that we cannot live a life in which we do everything correctly. If you did contribute to your financial downfall by foolish financial practices, repent of them and make yourself accountable to do better, then accept His forgiveness and walk in His freedom.

If you reach a place in your life where you are blessed financially, and you feel God is leading you to do so, you can repay bankruptcies even after they are settled in the courts. Doing so, or even attempting to do it, is a testimony of your integrity and a witness to others.

∾ *The wicked borrows and does not pay back, but the righteous is gracious and gives. (Psalms 37:21)*
∾ *If we confess our sins, He is faithful and righteous to forgive us our sins and to cleanse us from all unrighteousness. (1 John 1:9)*

∾

12. Our adult son and his wife have overspent for the first five years of their marriage. Now they wish to borrow enough money from us to pay off their debt. They are offering to repay it, but would we be wise to do this?

*F*irst of all, God seems to encourage the practice of giving money rather than lending money to others, whether

216

it is within the Christian family or blood relatives. However, in following God's instruction to be wise stewards of our belongings, there are several factors to look at before you make a decision. The most important one is whether or not you and your husband can afford to give the money to your son. It would not be good to endanger your financial security in order to make your son's finances better. You state that you feel that their lack of money stems from overspending. Therefore, you may be wondering if a loan will not solve the core issue of financial mismanagement. Depending on how open your relationship is, perhaps you could help them set up a budget or offer to pay for credit counseling for them before agreeing to help them financially.

You also do not mention whether your son and his wife have a family. You would not want children to go without food or necessities when it is in your power to offer aid. The best course of action will be for you to pray about it and let God direct you into a decision that you both can agree upon. In many ways our children remain a responsibility as long as we live, and therefore sometimes we give help simply because they are family and need it; not because they deserve it.

~ You shall freely open your hand to him, and shall generously lend him sufficient for his need in whatever he lacks. (Deuteronomy 15:8)

~ But whoever has the world's goods, and sees his brother in need and closes his heart against him, how does the love of God abide in him? (1 John 3:17)

~

13. I find a budget too confining and have never had one I have stuck to. Is there something I am doing wrong?

*T*here may be several things. The first is that your budget may not be realistic. A budget is a spending plan, and you may not be including every type of spending that is a part of your lifestyle. It may also be that your budget is pointing out the fact that you are not disciplined in your spending, and you need to get serious about your spending habits.

The reason for a budget is twofold: to free you to accomplish your financial goals and to give you peace of mind. Living on a budget is a good tool for teaching your children fiscal responsibility. However, if you cannot do it; you cannot teach it.

∾ *The mind of man plans his way, but the LORD directs his steps. (Proverbs 16:9)*

∾ *I have learned how to get along happily whether I have much or little. (Philippians 4:11 NLT)*

∼

14. How can I tell if money is my god?

*Y*ou can examine how important having, acquiring, and spending money is to your happiness. Is your security tied to money? Do you spend a lot of time thinking about money— ways to save it, ways to spend it, ways to get more? Are you impressed by other people's belongings, and consider that "things" constitute success? Financial advisor Larry Burkett lists three other warning signs that money may control you:

- You spend an inordinate amount of time pursuing financial success (and probably are not satisfied at any time with the level you have achieved).
- You spend your money on yourself and other selfish pursuits.
- There is dissatisfaction in your life, which drives you to spend more time pursuing financial success.

∾ *It is vain for you to rise up early, to retire late, to eat the bread of painful labors. (Psalms 127:2)*

∾ *But those who want to get rich fall into temptation and a snare and many foolish and harmful desires which plunge men into ruin and destruction. For the love of money is a root of all sorts of evil, and some by longing for it have wandered away from the faith and pierced themselves with many griefs. (1 Timothy 6:9–10)*

~

15. My eighteen-year-old has already received two credit card offers in the mail. How can I be confident that my kids will understand the pitfalls that credit cards hold?

The Bible speaks much about handling money responsibly. Therefore, in helping your child learn to live in the twenty-first century, I believe you will teach him best by allowing him to use one. Allow him to have one credit card. Agree together on what it can be used for and that the balance must be paid in full each month. The first time it does not get paid in its entirety, he will lose it until it is paid, plus for three additional months.

When he gets his statement, sit down together and explain it. Show him how much money he loses each time it is not paid in full. The miracle of monthly installments is very deceiving, so show him how costly that $15 tank of gas is over a six-month period.

∾ *My son, let them not vanish from your sight; keep sound wisdom and discretion. (Proverbs 3:21)*

∾ *Beware, and be on your guard against every form of greed. (Luke 12:15)*

16. In a recent conversation with friends, we discovered that they feel that Christians should not have a savings account as that is hoarding and shows unbelief in God's provision. We've always considered saving wise. Are we wrong?

No, you are not wrong. Your friend's thinking is an example of my husband's maxim that "a strength carried to an extreme is a weakness." They are right in saying that hoarding is wrong. The motive behind such a practice says, "I can save enough to take care of myself." It is self-centered and shows no dependence on God. However, the fact that you have a savings account is not the same as hoarding. Saving is demonstrated by the old proverb that commends the ant for storing and gathering for the winter. Saving as a regular part of your life is a wise way to provide for future spending and emergencies. This habit is commended in Scripture. Like so much in Christianity, the focus needs to be on balance and glorifying God.

∾ *There is a grievous evil which I have seen under the sun: riches being hoarded by their owner to his hurt. (Ecclesiastes 5:13)*
∾ *But godliness actually is a means of great gain when accompanied by contentment. For we have brought nothing into the world, so we cannot take anything out of it either. (1 Timothy 6:6–7)*

∼

17. My husband is the sweetest man alive. He would give the shirt off his back to anyone in need, but when he gives away money that we need to provide food and pay bills for our family, I have a problem with him doing it. How can I make him see that he needs to think twice before just handing out money?

I am assuming you have tried to speak to him about this issue. Does he feel that you do not ever wish to help others? Is it possible to set a certain limit in the monthly budget for charitable giving? If nothing you've tried seems reasonable to him, I'd approach your pastor or an older man your husband respects and ask him to speak to him regarding it.

Has he been able to tell you why he always wants to give even when you do not have the money? Maybe it feeds his ego to be Mr. Generous. Sometimes people believe that giving makes them more acceptable to God, when nothing we do can add or detract from the love God has for us.

Maybe you need to widen his perspective on giving and show him that it does not have to be monetary. Instead, maybe he could volunteer at a food bank or become a Big Brother to a child.

∾ *Many will seek the favor of a generous man, and every man is a friend to him who gives gifts. (Proverbs 19:6)*
∾ *If anyone does not provide for his relatives and especially for his immediate family, he has denied the faith and is worse than an unbeliever. (1 Timothy 5:8 NIV)*

∼

18. I was raised in very financially lean circumstances. Now that I am married and my husband has a good job you would think I wouldn't worry about every penny, but I still do. Do you think I'll ever relax and feel financially secure?

Y ou will feel secure only when you realize the truth that your security comes from God. You may not realize that the source of your fear is not that you are afraid you'll end up poor again, it is that you do not believe God will take care of you. Feeling financially secure in today's economy is a vapor, because, as the nightly news demonstrates, anything can happen to our money. Therefore, do not chase feeling financially secure but instead pursue a relationship and dependence on God, who is the only real security in our life.

    I have been young and now I am old, yet I have not seen the righteous forsaken or his descendants begging bread. (Psalms 37:25)

    Be anxious for nothing, but in everything by prayer and supplication with thanksgiving let your requests be made known to God. (Philippians 4:6)

~

19. My husband is very stingy. He never wants to help others or give me spending money. What can I do?

Stinginess is actually a spiritual problem. You need to pray for God to open your husband's spiritual eyes. Salvation means making Jesus Lord of our life. When we are born again, we agree to surrender everything, including our finances, to His direction. This truth needs to become real to your husband, but it is not your responsibility, or place, to teach it. When he understands that everything he owns belongs to God, and that he will give an account for how he handles it, he will be more open to the leading of the Holy Spirit and the direction of the Scriptures to openhandedness and generosity.

Nevertheless, his miserliness does not mean you still cannot give. You can be open handed toward others with your time and talents. If you have a gift for sewing or baking, you can bless others with the work of your hands. You can be hospitable to those who come into your home, showing them honor. Generosity can be exhibited in many ways, so indulge yourself wholeheartedly in every avenue available.

❧ *The generous man will be prosperous, and he who waters will himself be watered. (Proverbs 11:25)*

❧ *No one can serve two masters; for either he will hate the one and love the other, or he will be devoted to one and despise the other. You cannot serve God and wealth. (Matthew 6:24)*

∼

20. What's the difference in tithes and offerings, and how should churches collect money?

The word *tithe* means "tenth." The Bible teaches that the first 10 percent of everything that God has given to us belongs to Him. Offerings are gifts (monetary or otherwise) that we give out of our abundance in worship to God for His provision to us. Generally we are to bring our tithe and our offerings to church each week to give them to God. Giving to God is an act of worship, not a penance, and should be celebrated.

The Bible directs us to bring our tithes to the storehouse, which would be designated our church, for just as a storehouse contains food for our body, so does a local church provide spiritual food for our souls. This fund pays the pastor of the church, the church expenses, plus any charitable giving that the church undertakes or is responsible for, such as caring for those within their body who are in need.

❧ *Bring your whole tithe into the storehouse that there may be food in my house. (Malachi 3:10 NIV)*

❧ *Each man should give what he has decided in his heart to give, not reluctantly or under compulsion, for God loves a cheerful giver. (2 Corinthians 9:7 NIV)*

21. When I see so many people struggling financially, I feel guilty over my success. It seems that everything I do prospers. Could I be deceiving myself and really be like the rich young ruler?

*B*eing rich is not a sin, just as being poor is not a sign of godliness. Truthfully, money is a neutral object only gaining worth by how we view it. In the Old Testament, one of the signs of God's blessings on someone was financial prosperity. Note Abraham and Job as two examples of godly men who were very wealthy. In the New Testament that is not always the case; God seemed to bless in other ways also, and financial security was not a dependable indication of God's approval.

However, there's no doubt that God does financially bless some people, so there is no reason to feel guilty over it. If you consistently examine yourself spiritually, hold your wealth lightly, and share with others less fortunate (two important aspects of handling wealth correctly), rejoice in this blessing.

∾ *In everything that he undertook . . . he sought his God and worked whole-heartedly. And so he prospered. (2 Chronicles 31:21 NIV)*
∾ *And my God will supply all your needs according to His riches in glory in Christ Jesus. (Philippians 4:1)*

TIME MANAGEMENT

1. Between family, work, and church, I do not have any time for myself. Is there a solution?

While it is probably true that you do not have any time for yourself, it is pretty essential that you find it before you totally collapse. Overextending ourselves seems to be an American phenomenon. We overspend, overcommit, and overeat. The Bible speaks of moderation. Analyze what your obligations are. At certain times, all of our lives get overloaded. If it is a lifestyle, the problem is usually not having learned how to say *no*.

Everyone needs time to regenerate. For myself, I consider 10 P.M. and beyond to be "Mom's time" and fiercely guard it. Woe to my kids if, after I put them to bed, they decide they need a drink of water or to speak to me. Everyone needs space in which to recharge his or her batteries. Ask for your husband's insight, examine your obligations closely, and carve out some time for yourself. At some point, if you do not, your health will insist on it.

∾ *There is an appointed time for everything. And there is a time for every event under heaven. For there is a proper time and procedure for every delight. (Ecclesiastes 8:6)*
∾ *Therefore there is now no condemnation for those who are in Christ Jesus. (Romans 8:1)*

∼

2. I know that volunteer work is important, but how can I find the time?

You need to keep two truths in mind. The first is that you cannot do everything all the time. Certain times of your life allow more flexibility than others. The childrearing years are all-consuming, but they do not last forever. If you are in the midst of raising toddlers, give yourself some slack. The second truth is that you may need to rethink your definition of *volunteer*. If you do not have time to regularly volunteer, consider doing it one day a month—such as being a relief for a regular worker at the food bank. Perhaps you might volunteer to oversee one yearly event such as the fall drive to help senior citizens winterize their homes. Maybe you can head up the yearly charitable clothing drive at work.

Above all, do not load yourself with guilt for what you see as a failure on your part. If we are willing to listen for God's prompting, He will show us when He has a task for us to do, and until that time, do not fret about it.

∾ *For there is a proper time and procedure for every delight. (Ecclesiastes 8:6)*
∾ *You shall do what is right and good in the sight of the LORD, that it may be well with you. (Deuteronomy 6:18)*

∾

3. Sunday is my only day for my family. Aren't I honoring God by devoting myself to my family? Do I really need church?

*A*n amazing principle is if we do the first things first, there will be time for the second things. We can trust God to multiply our time if we honor Him by giving Him the first fruits. To answer your question, no, you are not honoring God if you put your family first. God is a jealous God. He will not play second place to anything or any person. By saying your family is the most important priority, you have made them something you worship. The First Commandment speaks to that sin. Remember the saying, "A man is never so tall as when he stoops to help a child"? In the same way, you will never demonstrate your love for your family better than when you worship God, for out of that worship will come greater devotion to your family. It is a win/win situation.

∾ *Give to the LORD the glory he deserves! Bring your offering and come to worship him. Worship the LORD in all his holy splendor. (1 Chronicles 16:29 NLT)*

∾ *Not forsaking our own assembling together, as is the habit of some, but encouraging one another; and all the more, as you see the day drawing near. (Hebrews 10:25)*

~

4. I simply cannot make myself stick to a schedule. Is that important?

Yes, the Bible does indicate that our life has purpose and we need to live it deliberately and productively. Ecclesiastes assures us that there is a time for everything, but by failing to plan we will rob ourselves of productive time and fail to accomplish our goals. A schedule is important for all areas of life. Sometimes we incorrectly believe that a schedule is only for chores and work. Therefore we assume that creating a schedule will simply result in more drudgery and preclude having any fun. Nothing could be further from the truth. A schedule, whether detailed or general, lets you see clearly how you spend your time. It allows you to make sure your life is balanced. Is there time for work and play? Do I go long periods between recreation? A schedule, like all rules, sets us free. It does not stifle spontaneity. A schedule is not to be a taskmaster, but rather a guideline or outline of what we wish to accomplish. While schedules often change (and if we are wise, we write appointments in pencil), at least they head us in the right direction. It is a tool to help us evaluate where we have been and where we are going.

∾ *He who tills his land will have plenty of food, but he who follows empty pursuits will have poverty in plenty. (Proverbs 28:19)*
∾ *Teach me good judgment and knowledge. (Psalms 119:66 NLT)*

~

5. Are overachievers more spiritual?

*N*ot at all. At least they are not more spiritual because of it. However, some may have strong spiritual attributes because of the character they have developed in their lives. In order to believe the "more is better" reasoning, you have to believe that our efforts of accomplishment make God look upon us more kindly.

In actuality, nothing we do can add or take away from God's love for us. His love is full and complete and, unlike our love, does not waver according to our response or non-response. There are several reasons that the extent of our accomplishments does not make a difference to our spiritual worth. One is that our best efforts of righteousness still appear as trash when compared to God's glory. Second, if we could in some way earn our way to Heaven, then Jesus died in vain for our sins.

∾ *"But with everlasting loving kindness I will have compassion on you," says the LORD your Redeemer. (Isaiah 54:8)*
∾ *For by grace you have been saved through faith; and that not of yourselves, it is the gift of God; not as a result of works, so that no one may boast. (Ephesians 2:8–9)*

6. Everyone agrees daily devotions are important, but I cannot find the time.

*T*ime is a commodity that everyone has the same amount of, and yet is it true that some seem to accomplish more with their time than others do. What's the key? In everything, we need to give God the first fruits. If you will begin your day by spending time with God, your productivity in the remainder of the day will appear as if you've received extra time. There is a hidden truth that God multiplies anything you give to Him first. Whether it is money or time, God has a way of making the remainder go farther if we'll honor Him with it first.

Some of us find that early in the morning is not a good time for us to do anything. In others words, since I cannot make conscious decisions before 9 A.M., my method has been to end my day with devotions, knowing that God will use my sleeping hours to commune with me. I wake up more refreshed and without the need to concentrate before my engine actually gets started.

❧ *Blessed is the man who listens to me, watching daily at my gates, waiting at my doorposts. (Proverbs 8:34)*
❧ *In the early morning, while it was still dark, Jesus got up, left the house, and went away to a secluded place, and was praying there. (Mark 1:35)*

~

7. The age-old argument about quality versus quantity regarding anything of value rages on. Is it true that how we spend our time defines our priorities?

I really like being decisive, so the answer is *yes* . . . and *no*. In most areas I would have to say that you are comparing apples and oranges when you try to show minute-by-minute that where you spend your time equals what you value most. If that were true, sleep would probably end up being something we most value. When in actuality, I doubt if that is true; rather it is a necessity for good health. Second, a great majority of women work out of the home each day due to financial necessity and those hours probably do not represent a true indication of their priorities.

A better criterion is to look at our leisure hours, our expendable time, and see how we spend those hours. If we have a family but all our free time is spent on our own hobby, even though hobbies are very important in themselves, it may rightly be assumed that hobbies are more important than family. Our finances may also speak to our priorities more clearly. If excessive extra money goes to our hobby or personal pleasure, then it may be a good indication that money is very important to us.

Instead of rating your priorities lineally or numerically, see your life as a wheel. Place God at the hub, or center, of the wheel and see the spokes as different areas of your life that flow out of your worship of God in the center. I may spend many more hours keeping house than I think is important, but I do it out of worship to God to serve my family. When work demands overtime, I see my attention to that duty as an extension of my worship to God and being a good employee.

~ *Seek his will in all you do, and he will direct your paths. (Proverbs 3:6 NLT)*
~ *Wherever your treasure is, there your heart and thoughts will also be. (Luke 12:34 NLT)*

~

8. I see articles all the time about women with four kids, a full-time career, who invent doodads they sell on weekends

at fairs, plus volunteer three nights a week at the homeless shelter, and I go home wondering what's wrong with me. I can barely manage two kids and a part-time job. Why am I not that productive?

*T*he nonsense that we can do everything in our life has caused more than one nervous breakdown. When we choose to do something with our time or money; we also choose *not* to do other things. We are wiser to manage our lives for the long haul. Sometimes we need to examine our motives. Are we trying to impress others with our capabilities? Do we realize the emotional cost to ourselves and our family when we cannot say no?

It is in this scenario that I more readily believe that quality is more important than quantity. The quality of a peaceful life, concentrating on just one or two important people/goals is much more appealing than trying to cram as many accomplishments as possible into our schedule.

I feel that many women fall into the trap of being people pleasers, rather than pleasing God. We need to know whom we serve. Do we serve men and become prey to social pressures to do it all and be all? What has God called you to? Seek His will for your life and He will lay the commitments on your heart that He wants you to fulfill.

& *There is an appointed time for everything. And there is a time for every event under heaven. (Ecclesiastes 3:1)*

& *Trust in the LORD with all your heart and do not lean on your own understanding. In all your ways acknowledge Him, and He will make your paths straight. (Proverbs 3:5–6)*

9. I cannot seem to keep a clean house. I am not talking about messy; I am talking dirty. What's the matter with me?

I do not imagine anything is the matter with you. Your dirty house can be attributed to any one of several things of which lack of training, lack of discipline, or lack of interest are a few. Ecclesiastes encourages us to do our best for the responsibilities that are ours, when it says, "Whatever your hand finds to do, do it with all your might" (9:10). I read somewhere that the difference between a clean house and a dirty house is one hour a day. It made a difference in my habits. I didn't think I could keep my house clean either (and by many people's standards it probably is still not clean), but I did know I could devote one hour each day to cleaning.

Sometimes we do not clean because the condition of it right now is too overwhelming to tackle. Maybe you need to call upon your sisters to come and help you gain control of the chaos first. The problem may stem from having too many belongings and being unable to put everything away. Truthfully, you do not need all those empty cottage cheese cartons, or if you do for freezing leftovers and berries in the summer, keep them in a box in the garage.

It is always good to have a plan of action. For example, if you tell yourself that you cannot go anywhere or do anything else each day until the Big 4 are accomplished, that may help set your day in order. What are the Big 4?—(1) dishes done, (2) beds made, (3) one load of laundry started, and (4) one other regular chore such as vacuuming, cleaning the bath, or dusting.

Another good trick is to end the day by picking up the rooms, emptying the dishwasher, and making sure the clothes in the dryer are folded and put away. Following a few basic guidelines will ensure that you will be on your way to a tidier home.

Finally, utilize those munchkin-size people in your house. Children as young as three can put away silverware from the dishwasher, empty trashcans, and certainly pick up their own toys.

If indeed your home is as bad as you would have us believe, I caution you not to set your standards too high too soon. If you expect perfection from the "get-go," you'll become discouraged and throw it all away.

∾ *Commit your work to the LORD and then your plans will be established. (Proverbs 16:3)*
∾ *Mark out a straight path for your feet. (Hebrews 12:13 NLT)*

~

10. I am a working mother with two preschoolers and a six-year-old. Mealtimes are chaos and usually consist of either soup and sandwiches or pizza delivered in. I know I am not teaching good nutrition. Can you give me any help?

I read one time that Ethyl Kennedy, sister-in-law of former President Kennedy and mother of eight children, only used three weeks' worth of menus all year long. When the twenty-first meal was served, it was time to go back to the beginning. I figured if three weeks was good enough for her blue blood, then it was certainly good enough for the Hildreths. So, in the spirit of looking well to your household as Proverbs encourages us, sit down one evening and plan out twenty-one meals that you like. Then, attach to each menu a copy of the recipe and a shopping list. Each week, take the shopping list and get everything you'll need at the store for that week's worth of meals. Repeat trips to the grocery store are not only a time waster, studies have also proved that those impromptu trips cost you plenty dollar-wise because of impulse shopping. Each night before you go to bed, check the next day's menu, take out any frozen meat you'll need, and place it in the refrigerator to thaw. When you know what you will be fixing and that you have all the ingredients right on hand, you will not find mealtimes so daunting.

That being said, remember that the focus of mealtimes is for families to be together, not the food. Peanut butter and jelly sandwiches are a healthier and cheaper choice than fast food.

∾ *She looks well to the ways of her household, and does not eat the bread of idleness. (Proverbs 31:27)*
∾ *Each of the younger women must be sensible and kind, as well as a good homemaker. (Titus 2:4–5 CEV)*

~

11. Tell me something good about ironing (and maybe I'll get around to doing mine).

*M*y feelings about ironing are probably equal to yours and you no doubt would appreciate Phyllis Diller's way of dealing with this duty: "I buried a lot of my ironing in the backyard." But mundane chores can be a veritable wealth of investing in others through prayer. While ironing, pray for the person whose garment you are ironing. Do not make them lip-service platitudes but ask for wisdom so you can see them through God's eyes. Pray for their protection, and ask God to give them purpose for their life and the determination to accomplish it. If the garment is one of your child's, pray for protection and guidance for her future mate. It is never too early to begin praying for such important people who will impact your family forever. If it is your garment, pray for spiritual eyes to discern your impact on the family. Pray for your husband's health, for guidance for his steps as he goes about his work.

You can carry this through in other work you do around the house: You can pray for missionaries while you vacuum, pray for your extended family as you do dishes. Face it, you can do your chores with your mind on neutral or you can redeem the time and use it wisely.

∽ *She watches over the affairs of her household and does not eat the bread of idleness. (Proverbs 31:27 NIV)*
∽ *Therefore be careful how you walk, not as unwise men but as wise, making the most of your time, because the days are evil. (Ephesians 5:15–16)*

∼

12. I like to do things right, but because that is so important to me, I cannot seem to get everything done that I should. How can I manage my time better?

Your problem is not that you need to learn to manage your time better. It is that you need to accept your less-than-perfect work. Telling someone to do something right is an okay directive for most people. However, to a perfectionist doing something right is really doing it *perfectly* and *my way*.

Perfectionism is a curse in our society and is an improper response to God's grace. Until you can accept that you are not perfect, that you do fall short, that you do need God's grace, you will not be able to accept yourself and your efforts.

Perfectionism is actually pride—the feeling of "I can do this." You look down on others whom you consider sloppy, and it makes you feel superior. Your perfectionism is a chain around your neck, keeping you from accepting God's grace extended to you. God looks at our heart and He is pleased with a gentle contrite spirit. Satan wants you bound by expectations that are unobtainable.

∽ *The Spirit of the Lord GOD is upon me . . . To proclaim liberty to captives and freedom to prisoners. (Isaiah 61:1)*
∽ *It is for freedom that Christ has set us free. Stand firm, then, and do not let yourselves be burdened again by a yoke of slavery. (Galatians 5:1 NIV)*

WORLD AND COMMUNITY

1. Why does the United States continue to give support to Israel? It seems Israel is causing a lot of problems in the Middle East.

I do not presume to know all the political reasons our government supports Israel. I am just very glad they do. I do know that ceasing to show friendship to them will reap our country disastrous consequences. The Bible says that the Jews are God's chosen people. Those who show them kindness will reap benevolence from God while those who demonstrate enmity will reap God's wrath. The land described in the Bible as the Promised Land was promised to Isaac's seed (present-day Jews), not Ishmael's seed (present-day Arabs). Because America is a democratic nation, we have trouble thinking in any terms other than majority rule. However, God does not operate democratically but rather theocratically. God deliberately chose the Jews as His people, and we have to be willing to trust God's omniscient decision. I am not saying that God loves the Arabic countries any less. His love toward them is the same as toward everyone. He desires a relationship with each of their citizens just as He does us. However, the physical land and the Jewish people hold a special place in His heart and we are warned never to turn against them.

❧ *The LORD said to Abram, after Lot had separated from him, "Now lift up your eyes and look from the place where you are, northward and southward and eastward and westward; for all the land which you see, I will give it to you and to your descendants forever. I will make your descendants as the dust of the earth, so that if anyone can number the dust of the earth, then your descendants can also be numbered. Arise, walk about the land through its length and breadth; for I will give it to you." Then Abram moved his tent and came and dwelt by the oaks of Mamre, which are in Hebron, and there he built an altar to the LORD. (Genesis 13:14–18)*

❧ *And the Scripture, foreseeing that God would justify the Gentiles by faith, preached the gospel beforehand to Abraham, saying, "All the nations will be blessed in You." (Galatians 3:8)*

~

2. Do I have any responsibility toward our governmental leaders?

*W*e are specifically directed to pray for our leaders. We sometimes take this charge lightly, often believing that direct involvement in politics is what is important. However, the Bible is full of changes that were brought about when God's people prayed. For example, Queen Esther is someone whose prayers saved an entire nation. It is easy to be apathetic over government decisions, assuming we are powerless to derail the huge governmental machinery, but when we align ourselves with God we are mighty.

In order to see the importance of our prayers, we need to understand that there are evil principalities whose sole purpose is to control entire countries through their leadership. It is not an exaggeration to say that world leaders are under spiritual attack constantly. They may not be aware that there are powers of darkness at work in their lives, but Christians are not to be so naive. Make a prayer list of your city, county, state, and national leaders. Bring the decisions they are debating before God every day and ask for His guidance. One practical way to do this is to take your daily newspaper and pray about each headline.

❧ *When the righteous increase, the people rejoice, but when a wicked man rules, people groan. (Proverbs 29:2)*
❧ *First of all, then, I urge that entreaties and prayers, petitions and thanksgivings, be made on behalf of all men, for*

kings and all who are in authority, so that we may lead a tranquil and quiet life in all godliness and dignity. This is good and acceptable in the sight of God our Savior. (1 Timothy 2:1–3)

~

3. Since God's will is ultimately going to be done anyway, why should I vote?

Voting is an act of accepting responsibility for our country. It is identifying with our nation and indicating we care about its future and wish to have a say in the decisions we make. In a practical way, it is one method that helps combat the feelings of powerlessness and cynicism we often feel at the seeming indifference of leaders toward the individual. God has never advocated that we ignore governmental authority; rather, He has stressed our responsibility to serve them to the best of our ability.

One of the greatest problems in America's political process is the lack of voter turnout. When we neglect to vote, we throw away a chance to make a difference. In the 2000 presidential election, the outcome of Florida's vote was held in abeyance for several weeks because of the closeness of the voter turnout. This would not have been an issue had either side more solidly turned out to vote. You cannot complain about our government if you have not taken advantage of your opportunity to vote.

The PBS Web site has written about the power of one vote in the following way.

What a Difference One Vote Makes

1820: One vote kept President James Monroe from being elected president.

1845: One vote made Texas one of the United States.

1846: One vote decided on war with Mexico.

1867: One vote gave the United States the state of Alaska.

1868: One vote saved President Andrew Johnson from being removed from office.

1876: One vote gave Rutherford B. Hayes the presidency of the United States.

1916: One vote in each of the voting areas of California re-elected President Wilson.

1948: One vote per precinct gave Truman the presidency.

1960: One vote per precinct would have elected Richard Nixon rather than John F. Kennedy president.

Now the leaders of the people lived in Jerusalem, but the rest of the people cast lots to bring one out of ten to live in Jerusalem, the holy city, while nine-tenths remained in the other cities. (Nehemiah 11:1)

And they drew lots for them, and the lot fell to Matthias; and he was added to the eleven apostles. (Acts 1:26)

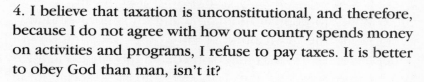

4. I believe that taxation is unconstitutional, and therefore, because I do not agree with how our country spends money on activities and programs, I refuse to pay taxes. It is better to obey God than man, isn't it?

*A*ctually, while this is a popular thought among some Christian separatists, the Sixteenth Amendment to the Constitution clearly states that paying taxes is our legal duty. The disciples evidently were pondering the advisability of paying taxes to their egregious leaders, but when they brought the matter to Jesus, He told them to obey the law. God sets up governments. He rules through a chain of authority, even ungodly authority. He instructs us to obey the laws of our land, and withholding our taxes is clearly an act of disobedience.

While it is true you may not agree with many of the decisions your government makes, you can remember and give thanks for blessings they have made possible such as public education or the police and fire departments.

❧ *So Jehoiakim gave the silver and gold to Pharaoh, but he taxed the land in order to give the money at the command of Pharaoh. He exacted the silver and gold from the people of the land, each according to his valuation, to give it to Pharaoh Neco. (2 Kings 23:35)*

❧ *Then render to Caesar the things that are Caesar's; and to God the things that are God's. (Matthew 22:21)*

~

5. Our Constitution requires the separation of church and state, so why are Christians so outspoken about bringing religious observances into the public arena?

There are many misconceptions regarding what the phrase *separation of church and state* means. First of all, contrary to popular thought, that term is not found anywhere in the Constitution, nor the Declaration of Independence. Thomas Jefferson coined this phrase in a letter he composed to the Danbury Baptist Association in Connecticut. In it he voiced his concern that great care should be taken to see that government did not stifle the free expression of religious worship.

A second reason our freedom of worship should be visible is because it is our historical heritage. If we don't know where we came from, we will not know where we are going. All historical documents give strength to the truth that America was founded upon godly principles and that they encouraged the free worship of God.

I am at a loss to discover why you believe that Christianity is to be lived out only in the private sector. People of moral integrity can be a positive influence wherever they are. Esther, Joseph, and Daniel are examples of God-fearing people whose lives benefited the ungodly nations in which they lived.

∾ *Blessed is the nation whose God is the LORD. (Psalms 33:12)*
∾ *First, I thank my God through Jesus Christ for you all, that your faith is being proclaimed throughout the whole world. (Romans 1:8)*

~

6. I see so many impoverished countries in the world. I am perplexed by the contrast between their standards of living and ours. Do you have any insights as to why we are so blessed?

Woven all through Scripture is the principle of sowing and reaping. America is a country that was established to allow the free worship of God. It is also one in which God figures prominently in its laws and governmental organization. Out of this heritage flows a generous heart. No other nation gives more of itself, its resources, and its people to help others than we do.

Another reason is that America continues to be a sending agency. We are a leading force in spreading the Great Commission as commanded by Jesus in Matthew, chapter 28, verses 19–20.

Sadly, I do not believe we are demonstrating the same godly principles in our national life now. We have strayed far from our heritage. For instance, we have taken prayer out of our schools, which is in direct contrast to the purpose of our first schools, which were established to teach about God and used the Bible as a primer. For years it was the practice to set aside one day a week for worship, with business closing so families and friends could be together. Evidence of corruption in government and business has to reach epic proportions before they are condemned.

However, because God is a merciful God, we are still reaping blessings from the good our forefathers sowed. We still enjoy financial prosperity. Even our very poorest are rich compared to citizens of Third World countries. We have the rights to move unhindered about our country, worship as we please, and the freedom to raise our families as we think best. I am positive we would see more of His blessings if, as a nation, we would turn our hearts back to the principles upon which this great nation was founded.

∾ *It is the blessing of the LORD that makes rich, and He adds no sorrow to it. (Proverbs 10:22)*
∾ *Instruct them to do good, to be rich in good works, to be generous and ready to share. (1 Timothy 6:18)*

∾

7. We are seeing an escalation of terrorism in the name of religion. What can I say when people seem to lump all religious people in the same pot?

You can emphatically state that destroying lives is not done in the name of the God. Neither is it done at His behest, because it is inconsistent with God's character. There is an old saying your mom may have quoted, which is "Your actions speak louder than your words." God is love. The actions of terrorists provide visible proof of a motive that is hateful and destructive. Do not be misled by rhetoric. There is only one true God, and His nature and ways are revealed in Scripture and are consistent with His character.

However, there is someone who epitomizes destruction. The Bible says Satan "comes to steal, kill and destroy" (John 10:10). If we look at the actions of terrorists, the evidence of death and destruction should bring us to the conclusion that their motives do not come from God.

∾ *You shall not worship their gods, nor serve them, nor do according to their deeds. (Exodus 23:24)*
∾ *For what do righteousness and wickedness have in common? Or what fellowship can light have with darkness? (2 Corinthians 6:14 NIV)*

∾

8. We read so much about random acts of violence both here and abroad. What has caused this modern phenomenon?

*O*ne reason we see more incidences of violence is that there is more media coverage today than ever before to make us aware of events.

However, Solomon said, "There is nothing new under the sun." Evil has existed since God created the world and there has always been violence since Cain killed his brother. However, true to the Bible's prediction in Matthew, chapter 24, evil has escalated. This is because we are living in what the Bible calls "the last days" when He said evil would abound. The reason for violence is that it is an outward reflection of an inner frustration. St. Augustine said that in each person there is a God-shaped vacuum that nothing except God can fill. Too often we try to satisfy a spiritual hunger by pursuing other seemingly fulfilling pursuits. Because it doesn't fill that void, our feeling of emptiness increases and heightens our frustration. In James, chapter 4, it says that strife occurs because we desire what others have;

in other words, we are greedy. And violence is the end result of this drive of envy and greed.

∿ *Cease from anger and forsake wrath; do not fret; it leads only to evildoing. (Psalms 37:8)*

∿ *But realize this, that in the last days difficult times will come. For men will be lovers of self, lovers of money, boastful, arrogant, revilers, disobedient to parents, ungrateful, unholy . . . (2 Timothy 3:1–2)*

∼

9. We recently had a march in our town by members of a certain religious faction who were spreading a hate-filled message against gays. They insisted that Scripture instructs them to be this hostile. I couldn't believe that was true except that when I searched the Scripture I found some pretty harsh words said about homosexuals. Are we to do as these verses say?

Simply put: No. One of the best methods of seeking truth is by researching to see where the burden of proof lies. In other words, *more is good*. The more Scriptures you have to give you guidance on an issue, the stronger your stand can be. A correlating truth is that we need to look at both the Old Testament and New Testament to get God's whole viewpoint.

In the Old Testament, under the Law, God had very strict rules and severe punishment for transgressors. Therefore, by taking isolated portions of Scripture, you can stir up hatred. However, using only isolated verses is a warning sign that you do not have the whole picture. If you were to live your life on isolated Scriptures, you would also believe that rebellious teens should be stoned to death and that if your neighbor accidentally injured you that you would have the right to inflict the same injury on him. This is not true. Heavy-duty verses, given under the Law, proved ineffectual in bringing mankind into right standing with God.

This is why Jesus Christ came to die. It was because meting out harsh punishment does not deal with the sin. We do not need a penalty. We need regeneration. The Bible designates anything that is contrary to God's Word as sin. This does include a homosexual lifestyle. It also includes hatred.

Those who focus their message on hating gays, rather than disapproving of the gay lifestyle, are in error themselves before God. God has always advocated extending love to those outside of His law.

∾ *Hatred stirs up strife, but love covers all transgressions. (Proverbs 10:12)*
∾ *But the one who hates his brother is in the darkness and walks in the darkness, and does not know where he is going because the darkness has blinded his eyes. (1 John 2:11)*

∾

10. I seem to get the impression from many Christians that to speak out against the homosexual lifestyle is wrong; instead, all we need to do is love them. This bothers me, but neither do I wish to be hateful. What should my attitude be toward homosexuality?

Whenever we are unsure of how we ought to proceed, it is important to remember our job description. Christ told us we are the salt of the world and a light set on a hill to offer guidance to those around. When opportunity presents itself to give an opinion, be ready to offer God's viewpoint. God wishes to offer hope to the unbeliever, not to condemn him. If a person never hears another perspective, they will not have any reason to examine their beliefs regarding it. A simple question such as, "Since God is love, why would He

247

condemn a practice that was inborn?" may give you a platform on which to discuss God's opinion.

What we are not called to do is win arguments, for "a man convinced against his will is unconvinced still" is a truism. There is a difference between expressing God's view on a subject and condemning a person. When discussing volatile issues, remember that everyone deserves to be treated as a person of value. No matter what their philosophy or lifestyle, they deserve dignity and respect. Each individual is created in God's image, and Christ died for him just as He did for you and me. Your attitude should be the same as Christ's was toward anyone caught in sin. He offered forgiveness and grace.

Pray for God to open doors for you to speak truth. Until He does, work on establishing relationships in order to have credibility. And when an opportunity is given, use the wisdom He has promised you to speak lovingly and without condemnation. Sadly, too often Christians have been guilty of throwing out the person along with the sin. It is no wonder that we, and our message, are sometimes disregarded.

∾ *If there is a man who lies with a male as those who lie with a woman, both of them have committed a detestable act. (Leviticus 20:13)*
∾ *But sanctify Christ as Lord in your hearts, always being ready to make a defense to everyone who asks you to give an account for the hope that is in you, yet with gentleness and reverence. (1 Peter 3:15)*

∼

11. My elementary and junior high children are asking many questions about everything happening in the Middle East. I know there are spiritual answers for these things, but they are complex and often scary. How much should I tell them?

*Y*ou can become informed and use their questions as a springboard to discuss foreign policy and the role America plays in world issues. You can also admit that you do not know all the answers, but that the bottom-line issue seems to be, who is going to control the Middle East. Share with them God's perspective on nations that support Israel, which is that He promises benefits to those who do and judgment on those who do not. Above all, assure them that even when everything seems chaotic, God is in control. He will walk with us through any situation we face in our lives.

Buy books on End Times teaching, and read them along with your Bible. In this way you will become educated on actions that will occur before Christ returns for His Church. Then use the newspaper headlines as a daily Bible/current events lesson.

∾ *The king's heart is like channels of water in the hand of the LORD; He turns it wherever He wishes. (Proverbs 21:1)*
∾ *He is before all things, and in Him all things hold together. (Colossians 1:17)*

∾

12. Since September 11, the Middle Eastern community in our town has endured quite a bit of vandalism to their property. It makes me sad, but I do wonder if we, as a nation, are harboring people who mean us harm?

*D*uring times of stress, logic often goes out the window. You probably do not hate all persons of German descent because of World War II or all Vietnamese in retaliation for Vietnam. America has always welcomed people from all cultures. In many towns where these same shameful acts occurred following September 11, citizens made a concerted effort to reach out to the Middle Eastern families. Students wrote letters of sympathy and sent gifts. They invited them to come to school and talk about why their family came to America. Ill-treatment based on ethnic origins catapults us back a century to our less-than-credible time of history.

Instead, pray and ask Almighty God who is "a discerner of the thoughts and intents of the heart" to reveal any evil plans. We certainly need to be alert for those who mean harm to our nation, and report any suspicious behavior, but do not side with the vigilantism.

∾ *The LORD nullifies the counsel of the nations; he frustrates the plans of the peoples. (Psalms 33:10)*
∾ *For the word of God is living and active and sharper than any two-edged sword, and piercing as far as the division of soul and spirit, of both joints and marrow, and able to judge the thoughts and intentions of the heart. And there is no creature hidden from His sight, but all things are open and laid bare to the eyes of Him with whom we have to do. (Hebrews 4:12–13)*

~

13. How do I teach my children to be aware of the needs of others?

Your best tool is the example of your life. Every time an ambulance goes by, pray for the people it is racing to help. At bedtime, pray that the homeless in your town will find a warm place to sleep. Be approachable to others' needs by being aware when a friend needs help with her children, cleaning her home, or carpooling, and offer your help. Find a need and fill it. In every instance possible include your children's assistance, because when they feel they are a part in serving it becomes more meaningful. Let them see the joy you get from serving others. Be open with them and talk about how good it feels to lend a helping hand. You will probably find that they will begin to have kind hearts and point out situations in which your family can show compassion.

꙳ *Whatever your hand finds to do, do it with your might. (Ecclesiastes 9:10)*
꙳ *Be devoted to one another in brotherly love; give preference to one another in honor. (Romans 12:10)*

~

14. I am an African-American living in an African-American community. How can I make friends with Caucasians and other ethnic groups?

Follow the advice of the old fisherman: To catch fish, go where the fish are. Step out of your comfort zone—take a night class or join a book club. If you are able, attend a church outside your neighborhood. Suggest going out for coffee to a couple of people or invite them over for your special meal. You will find others who also want to enlarge their horizons. Remember, kindness attracts others.

Different cultures have many wonderful traditions that would be fun to explore. Attend cultural fairs within your city to discover more about their heritage.

꙳ *A man who has friends must himself be friendly. (Proverbs 18:24 NKJV)*
꙳ *Be kind to one another [and] tender-hearted. (Ephesians 4:32)*

~

15. I am uncomfortable in public demonstrations against abortion. Is there anything else I can do to save babies?

We aren't all called to the same type of ministry. But we all must speak up for justice ("What does the Lord require of you but to do justice" [Micah 6:8]). You can write letters to the editor in the paper expressing your view on abortion. You can also write and phone your elected officials to let them know how you want them to vote. Another way is to volunteer at a Crisis Pregnancy Line or home for unwed mothers. And most important, in casual conversation with friends, coworkers and family, emphasize your sympathy for the plight of unborn children. Finally, use the power of your vote to vote for candidates with a pro-life platform.

∾ *Behold, children are a gift of the LORD, the fruit of the womb is a reward. (Psalms 127:3)*
∾ *And they were bringing children to Him so that He might touch them . . . and He took them in His arms and began blessing them, laying His hands on them. (Mark 10:13, 16)*

~

16. Can I make a difference in the lives of the poor in Africa?

Yes, we can be responsive to the poor. The Bible makes it abundantly clear that God has a special eye on the poor and unfortunate.

If you wish to help in a way that will make the greatest difference, do some research and become involved with an organization that enables Africans to help themselves. History demonstrates that relief aid is only a short-term remedy. It's the philosophy of "give a man a fish and you'll feed him for a day; teach him how to fish and you'll feed him for his life." You can best help by giving them a future. One good choice would be to adopt a child for schooling, because as citizens become educated they can work for a better Africa.

There are some good programs that have established

themselves over a period of years in Third World countries, and you can find a list of them in the bibliography.

❧ *He who oppresses the poor taunts his Maker, but he who is gracious to the needy honors Him. (Proverbs 14:31)*
❧ *Go and sell all you possess and give to the poor, and you will have treasure in heaven; and come, follow Me. (Mark 10:21)*

~

17. Should I be concerned about religious persecution in countries like China? If so, what should I do?

One of the hardest lessons for Christians to learn is that we are a global community—what affects a brother or sister elsewhere, affects us. First of all, pray for them. Remember, our enemy isn't people but Satan's influence in people's lives. Speak out in letters to the editor and to members of Congress about U.S. trade being linked to humane treatment of all China's citizens, Christians and non-Christians alike.

You can also check to see if your church does any missionary outreach that you could assist or become part of in China. Join with efforts to send Bibles and literature to Christians in China.

❧ *The LORD performs righteous deeds and judgments for all who are oppressed. (Psalms 103:6)*
❧ *Remember the prisoners, as though in prison with them, and those who are ill-treated, since you yourselves also are in the body. (Hebrews 13:3)*

18. Is there anything I can do to help single parents in my community?

*P*ersonal effort rather than an anonymous financial contribution is always more rewarding. Get involved by adopting a single-parent family you know in your community. Ask what they need and do what you can to provide it. This can involve your whole family or even your church. Being a single parent is the hardest job in the world, and they desperately need emotional support. When you align yourself with a single-parent household, your friendship provides support and protection. It is vital for children raised in a fatherless home to have good male role models in their lives. By inviting a special family over to dinner on a regular basis, the children can observe the importance of a mother or father's influence. Maybe the single parent needs the loan of your washer and dryer once a week to do her laundry; you can chat while the kids play and the clothes spin-dry. If it is a single mother, your husband can help with the upkeep on her vehicle or with emergency home repairs. Remember these folks at holidays, and offer to keep the kids overnight once a month to give the parent a break.

∾ *Two are better than one because they have a good return for their labor. For if either of them falls, the one will lift up his companion. But woe to the one who falls when there is not another to lift him up. Furthermore, if two lie down together they keep warm, but how can one be warm alone? And if one can overpower him who is alone, two can resist him. A cord of three strands is not quickly torn apart. (Ecclesiastes 4:9–12)*

∾ *Pure and undefiled religion in the sight of our God and Father is this: to visit orphans and widows in their distress, and to keep oneself unstained by the world. (James 1:27)*

19. Telephone solicitors, many of them representing fine civic organizations, regularly contact me. How can I decide which organization will use my money wisely?

Stewardship is a very important principle in the Bible. The story of the three servants who were entrusted with differing amounts of money to invest shows us that God expects us to handle wisely what he's entrusted to us. This means that we have a responsibility to check out any organization that we support with our money.

When a solicitor calls, and you think it is an organization you might be interested in supporting, request that last year's financial statement be sent to you. By looking at it you will have a better idea how much of your contribution will actually go to help their cause versus how much might be kept for overhead expenses.

There is a watchdog organization called ECFA (*www.ecfa.org*)—Evangelical Council for Financial Accountability—that rates charitable organizations according to how effectively they use the money donated to them. They publish an informational pamphlet that sets out a "Donor's Bill of Rights." Check with them regarding any ministry you are considering donating to.

∾ *The generous man will be prosperous. (Proverbs 11:25)*
∾ *Give an account of your stewardship. (Luke 16:2 NKJV)*

~

20. In our town, I am approached every day by one of the homeless for a handout. I hate it when I say *no*. But I do not believe in cash handouts either. What's the best way to help these people?

*A*lthough Scripture reminds us that doing good for others is the same as ministering to God, this is not a situation in which to let sympathy outweigh reality. In most cases, giving money to the homeless is not a good idea. Instead, give your financial support to the many fine organizations that provide food and shelter for them. These organizations always need financial support and are much better equipped to meet the needs of the homeless population.

If you wish to give personally, offer to accompany the homeless person to a local coffee shop and buy him or her a meal. If you encounter them frequently, purchase books of fast-food coupons that you can give them to redeem for a meal. You might purchase a takeout lunch and share it on a park bench in a highly visible public area while you tell him or her about Jesus' love for them—the best help of all you can give.

Get involved in community efforts that enable them to rebuild their lives, such as tutoring or job training.

But happy are those who have the God of Israel as their helper, whose hope is in the LORD their God. . . . He is the one who . . . gives justice to the oppressed and food to the hungry. (Psalms 146:5, 7 NLT)

I was hungry, and you gave Me something to eat; I was thirsty, and you gave Me something to drink; I was a stranger, and you invited Me in; naked, and you clothed Me; I was sick, and you visited Me; I was in prison, and you came to Me. (Matthew 25:35–36)

21. I am concerned about saving our planet. What is the best way to become involved?

*W*e need to have respect for God's creation and not wantonly destroy it. God gave to Adam the responsibility of the care of the Garden of Eden and that responsibility continues to us. How involved you get and just what ecological measures you adopt depends on your resources and time. Some of the easy and obvious choices are to recycle rather than throwing away, ride bikes, walk, or use public transportation. Wherever possible, if your budget can afford it, purchase products that have been produced under environmentally friendly conditions.

God instructed Adam that the earth and all that was in it was for man to use and enjoy. He made everything in the earth for man's benefit and enjoyment but not to be worshiped.

∾ *The earth is the LORD'S, and all it contains, the world, and those who dwell in it. (Psalms 24:1)*
∾ *Heaven and earth will pass away, but My words will not pass away. (Matthew 24:35)*

∾

22. How involved in the political process can a believer be?

There's a popular misconception today that the term "separation of church and state" means Christians do not belong in politics. Nothing could be further from the truth. Consider Nehemiah, the cup-bearer to the king, who used his position and influence to help restore Israel's kingdom. Daniel was the second-highest ranking official in the Babylonian empire and used it to serve God. As a citizen you have every right and a responsibility to become as involved as you have time for and enjoy doing. The greatest danger is the discouragement you'll face as a Christian in the political process. If you enter with the right motives, to rally for truth, you'll be doing a good thing. To follow Christ, we must fight for the cause of justice.

∾ *Now Joseph was the ruler over the land. (Genesis 42:6)*
∾ *For by Him all things were created, both in the heavens and on earth, visible and invisible, whether thrones or dominions or rulers or authorities—all things have been created through Him and for Him. (Colossians 1:16)*

∾

23. The city council wishes to place a juvenile home in my neighborhood. I am greatly disturbed about this. What would Christ want me to do?

I sense you feel guilty for opposing the facility, but one of the reasons God established families is to provide protection for vulnerable children and the elderly. Before a decision is made, there are many issues to be considered: Find out how secure the facility is and what type of juveniles will be housed in it. Will the city provide extra patrols in your area? What are the demographics of your neighborhood? All of this information will help you make an intelligent decision.

What is important is that you remember to keep your attitude correct. Christ would have us exhibit compassion for those outside the law. Not only is ranting and raving unchristian behavior, it will be self-defeating before the city council.

∾ *Don't be in a hurry to go to court. You might go down before your neighbors in shameful defeat. (Proverbs 25:8 NLT)*
∾ *He can have compassion on those who are ignorant and going astray. (Hebrews 5:2 NKJV)*

∾

24. My teenager wants to work with a charitable organization located in the inner city. All of a sudden social action

has come close to home and I am terrified. Am I wrong to say no?

*Y*es, you are wrong to say no, but you do need to do your homework. Check with the organization where he or she wishes to work and check out what safeguards and street-smart training they give their staff. By opposing his or her call to ministry, you are really saying God cannot take care of him. I understand your concern, but the stories of the Israelite maiden (2 Kings 5:1–4) and Daniel, Shadrach, Meshack, and Abednego (Daniel 34:13–30) have always comforted me as a parent. They are good reminders of God's care for our children. These parents had no choice where their children went, but they had prepared them by teaching them of the omnipresent, omnipotent God and trusted Him to protect them. On a practical note, make sure your teen is well trained in street smarts before going. Find out what kinds of safety measures the program offers volunteers. Above all, pray. The reality is that we have our children for such a short time, and we cannot protect them forever. We have to release them into God's care and trust. If we begin to do it from the time they are small, acknowledging daily that they belong to God, it will be easier to let them go when they're eighteen.

꙳ *In peace I will both lie down and sleep, for You alone, O LORD, make me to dwell in safety. (Psalms 4:8)*
꙳ *What then shall we say to these things? If God is for us, who is against us? (Romans 8:31)*

25. I own a home in what is becoming a multicultural low-income area with a growing gang presence. How can I keep my neighborhood safe?

igilance is protection. You can organize a block watch. Network in your neighborhood to find others who are concerned and get together to make a plan to protect your families, especially the children and elderly. Solicit help from law enforcement and area churches for training and support. Because of the increase of children being kidnapped in our society, in Seattle, Washington, one concerned mom organized a neighborhood school watch. When the children walk to the local elementary school each day, there is an adult standing outside in each block to watch their safe passage. This is one example of communities coming together to deal with the threat of danger to its citizens.

∽ *You shall keep the watch of the house, lest it be broken down. (2 Kings 11:6 NKJV)*
∽ *Behold, I send you out as sheep in the midst of wolves; so be shrewd as serpents and innocent as doves. (Matthew 10:16)*

∼

26. Test scores in the public schools in our area are low and the community seems apathetic. I foresee that my children will not be competitive in the job market when they graduate. Is there anything I can do short of enrolling them in a private school?

ou have identified a problem, so you need to address it. Talk to teachers and administration to see how they view the situation. Volunteer to be part of the educational quality committee to work on a plan for improvement. Become involved at the grassroots; talk to your local PTA about what needs to be done. Are classrooms large and too hard for one teacher to teach each student? Maybe the PTA needs to organize parent-volunteers to come in and tutor. The state government, which oversees the funding for all schools, needs to be brought into the discussion. Share your concerns with your legislators. Above all, do not accept it; be vocal in your quest because the squeaky wheel will be the one that gets the most attention.

One thing you can do is to make sure your children are readers. Read aloud to them, buy them books, and visit the library often. If they struggle with a class, find a high school student to tutor them. If you are not sure your school district's requirements are adequate, get on the Web and check out other school district's Web sites to see what grade-level standards they expect.

→ *For the LORD your God has blessed you in all that you have done. (Deuteronomy 2:7)*
→ *Therefore, my beloved brethren, be steadfast, immovable, always abounding in the work of the Lord, knowing that your labor is not in vain in the Lord. (1 Corinthians 15:57–58)*

27. I am a retired person who sees many latchkey kids wandering the neighborhood during the summer and after school. I feel they are at-risk children. Can I help?

*I*t is true that the most dangerous hours of a child's day is from 4 P.M. to 7 P.M., because that is the period of time in which they are out of school but before Mom or Dad gets home. During these three hours more juvenile crimes are committed than at any other time of day. So you are right in thinking that they are at-risk. Make friends with them and their families so they will feel safe in contacting you in case of an emergency or just to visit. You can always offer help with homework. A warm cookie at the end of a hard day of school and a listening ear is probably the best deterrent to juvenile crime you will find. Enlist the help of social organizations and churches in your area to begin after-school programs.

One word of caution: Do not make any overtures toward the children until you have made friends with the parents and have obtained their permission to speak to and invite their children into your home. Too many people are not as altruistic as they appear. Do not encourage children to make friends with you, a stranger, no matter how kindly your intentions, without contacting the parents first.

∾ *Better is a neighbor who is near than a brother far away.* *(Proverbs 27:10)*

∾ *So that you will walk in a manner worthy of the Lord, to please Him in all respects, bearing fruit in every good work.* *(Colossians 1:10)*

~

28. I've always considered euthanasia wrong, but I recently watched a friend lose his three-year battle with cancer. Observing what he endured, I am beginning to question whether it is not a reasonable choice for the terminally ill. Are there ever times when it would be okay to assist someone to die?

A well-known Christian commentator, Dr. James Dobson, calls this reasoning a "slippery slope." Let's play "what if" for a minute. What if it is okay to assist someone to die who is in the final throes of cancer—where does it end? They do not wish to end their lives anymore than a forty-year-old (or eighteen-year-old) bipolar sufferer who in her lowest depression pleads to be released from her emotional pit.

Emotional stress does not produce good decisions. Any subject can be couched in terms that make it sound acceptable. To decide what God's wishes are, we must first peel back the rhetoric and see what remains: Euthanasia is the deliberate act of taking someone's life.

The Sixth Commandment forbids murder. Only when we're willing to accede the sovereignty of life and death to God are we able to know what our decision should be. All of the arguments boil down to whether we accept our life as being by design and for a purpose or whether it is happenstance.

❧ *I have set before you life and death, the blessing and the curse. So choose life. (Deuteronomy 30:19)*
❧ *Do you not know that you are a temple of God and that the Spirit of God dwells in you? If any man destroys the temple of God, God will destroy him, for the temple of God is holy, and that is what you are. (1 Corinthians 3:16–17)*

~

29. Isn't eating the flesh of God's creatures wrong? I am thinking of becoming a vegetarian.

Choosing to or abstaining from eating meat is simply a matter of personal preference. It does not carry any spiritual meaning. God told Adam and Eve in the Garden of Eden that everything was created for man's enjoyment. Animal sacrifice was an important part of the atonement of God's people in the Old Testament. The only admonition in making your choice is not to let your practices offend others. Should you choose a vegetarian lifestyle, do not condemn people who choose not to join.

❧ *Then God said, "Behold, I have given you every plant yielding seed that is on the surface of all the earth, and every tree which has fruit yielding seed; it shall be food for you; and to every beast of the earth and to every bird of the sky and to every thing that moves on the earth which has life, I have given*

every green plant for food." (Genesis 1:29–30)
∾ *Eat whatever is sold in the meat market, without asking questions for conscience' sake; for the earth is the Lord's, and all it contains. (1 Corinthians 10:25–26)*

~

30. A friend in our church employs illegal immigrants on his farm. I feel this is wrong, but he just laughs about it. Does the Bible give us any guidelines?

*A*bsolutely. We are to follow the laws of our country. Rationalization has reared its ugly head again. The term *illegal* immigrants give us a clue that someone is abetting unlawful behavior. Having lived in agricultural communities a large portion of my life, I am well aware of this practice. First of all, it is wrong because it is against the law. Those who condone it contend that crops would rot in the fields if they didn't use illegal labor because Americans either refuse to do this menial work or they insist on higher wages. In Habakkuk, chapter 3, verses 17–18, it reads:

> Though the fig tree should not blossom and there be no fruit on the vines, though the yield of the olive should fail and the fields produce no food, though the flock should be cut off from the fold and there be no cattle in the stalls, yet I will exult in the LORD, I will rejoice in the God of my salvation.

If he would trust God for wisdom there is no doubt that God would make a way for him, just as he has for many farmers with whom I am acquainted who serve God and who have seen prosperity come because of their commitment to honesty.

❧ *See, I have set before you today life and prosperity, and death and adversity; in that I command you today to love the LORD your God, to walk in His ways and to keep His commandments and His statutes and His judgments, that you may live and multiply, and that the LORD your God may bless you in the land where you are entering to possess it. (Deuteronomy 30:15–16)*

❧ *He who is faithful in a very little [thing] is faithful also in much, and he who is dishonest and unjust in a very little [thing] is dishonest and unjust also in much. (Luke 16:10 AMP)*

❧

31. Do I have a responsibility as a Christian to do something about a friend of mine who is bragging about evading customs on her return from Europe?

No, you really do not. What she is doing is morally wrong and illegal, but it does not directly affect you, so you need to keep quiet. Pray for her that she will reconsider her behavior. All sin creates a wall between us and God and she needs that wall brought down and full communion with God re-established. Do not be drawn into discussions with others regarding her behavior. Keep yourself from sinning through gossip.

❧ *You shall not steal, or deal falsely, or lie to one another. (Leviticus 19:11)*

❧ *He who steals must steal no longer. (Ephesians 4:28)*

❧

32. I am upset because a registered sex offender just moved into our neighborhood. My husband says this is not a

Christian attitude, but I am worried about our elementary-school-aged children. What safeguards can I take?

I think both of your reactions are understandable. So now we need to see how we can put them together to make a workable solution. Your emotional response is a normal reaction to what you perceive as danger to the innocent citizens in your neighborhood—the children. A Christ-like attitude, which your husband wishes to exhibit would be to protect the helpless—again, the children.

Can I say that maybe you are safer knowing you have a sex offender who is identified than having one preying unbeknownst in your neighborhood? It is a reminder that you need to keep a close eye on your children and every child in the neighborhood. It would be good to reinforce the safety rules you have established for your children. They need to be reminded often that they are not to speak to strangers and that sometimes people who wish to harm them can appear friendly. I would make it a rule that they never walk in the neighborhood alone but always with a friend or sibling.

Above all, you can pray. Your neighbor has an eternal soul, and he needs God.

➣ *Rescue me, O LORD, from evil men; preserve me from violent men who devise evil things in their hearts. (Psalms 140:1–2)*

➣ *Whoever causes one of these little ones who believe in Me to stumble, it would be better for him to have a heavy millstone hung around his neck, and to be drowned in the depth of the sea. (Matthew 18:6)*

~

33. Can you tell me if there is a biblical stand on capital punishment? I am not sure what I believe regarding it.

*I*f the Bible has a view on capital punishment it seems to fall more toward accepting it than not. There are commands in the Old Testament regarding forfeiting your life if you have caused someone's death unjustly. That is because the Bible is a book of justice, and it understands that when sin is judged quickly it will keep it from spreading.

∾ *Because the sentence against an evil deed is not executed quickly, therefore the hearts of the sons of men among them are given fully to do evil. (Ecclesiastes 8:11)*
∾ *Now, will not God bring about justice for His elect who cry to Him day and night, and will He delay long over them? I tell you that He will bring about justice for them quickly. (Luke 18:7–8)*

BIBLIOGRAPHY

ADDICTIONS

Living with Your Husband's Secret Wars, Marsha Means. Fleming H. Revell, Co., 1999.

ADOLESCENCE

Adolescence Isn't Terminal (It Just Feels Like It), Kevin Leman. Tyndale House, 2002.

Breakaway Magazine, boys, ages twelve to fifteen (*www.family.org/teenguys/breakmag*).

Brio magazine, girls, ages twelve to fifteen (*www.brio mag.org*).

Emotionally Healthy Teenagers: Guiding Your Teens to Successful Independent Adulthood, Jay Kesler. Word Publishing, 1998.

Preparing for Adolescence: Caution, Changes Ahead, James C. Dobson. Gospel Light Publishing, 1999.

AGING

A Caregivers Survival Guide: How to Stay Healthy When Your Loved One Is Sick, Kay Marshall Strom. Intervarsity Press, 2000.

ANGER

Control Your Anger, Charles R. Swindoll. Insight for Christian Living, 1980; reprint, 1995.

Getting Anger under Control, Neil T. Anderson. Harvest House, 2002.

CHARITABLE ORGANIZATIONS IN AFRICA

Africa's Children—*www.africare.org*
Into Africa—*mcaninch@swiftkisumu.com*
Samaritan's Purse—*www.samaritanspurse.org*

COMMUNICATION

Communication: Key to Your Marriage, Norman H. Wright. Regal, 1974; reprint, 2000.

Incompatibility: Grounds for a Great Marriage!, Chuck and Barb Snyder. Multnomah, 1998.

The Two Sides of Love, Gary Smalley and John Trent. Focus on the Family, 1990.

DATING

Finding the Love of Your Life: 10 Principles for Choosing the Right Marriage Partner, Neil Clark Warren. Focus on the Family, 1992.

I Kissed Dating Goodbye, Joshua Harris. Multnomah, 1997.

Why True Love Waits, Josh McDowell. Tyndale House, 2002.

DEATH/GRIEF

Hope for the Troubled Heart, Dr. Billy Graham. Word Publishing, 1991.

Saying Goodbye When You Don't Want To: Teen's Dealing with Loss, Martha Bolton. Vine Books, 2002.

Surviving the Death of a Child, John Munday, Westminster John Knox Press, 1999.

EMOTIONS

Boundaries: When to Say Yes, When to Say No to Take Control of Your Life, Dr. Henry Cloud and Dr. John Townsend. Zondervan, 2002.

Dark Clouds, Silver Linings, Dr. Archibald Hart. Focus on the Family, 1993.

Emotions: Can You Trust Them?, Dr. James Dobson. Regal, 1981.

Managing Your Emotions, Joyce Meyer. Harrison House, 1997.

EVANGELISM

101 Ways to Reach Your Community, Steve Sjogren. NavPress, 2001.

FINANCES

Debt-Proof Living, Mary Hunt. Broadman & Holman, 1999.

Financial Guide for the Single Parent, Larry Burkett. Moody, 1997.

Taming the Money Monster: 5 Steps to Conquering Debt, Ron Blue. Focus on the Family, 1993.

GRANDPARENTING

Living the Lois Legacy: Passing on a Lasting Faith to Your Grandchildren, Helen Hosier. Tyndale House, 2002.

HOMESCHOOLING

www.k12.com

HOMOSEXUALITY

Children as Trophies: Examining the Evidence on Same-Sex Parenting, by Patricia Morgan. Christian Institute, 2002.

Helping People Step Out of Homosexuality, Frank Worthen. Regeneration Books, 1991.

Someone I Love Is Gay, Anita Worthen and Bob Davies. InterVarsity, 1996.

HOSPITALITY

A House of Many Blessings: A Christian Guide to Hospitality, Quin Sherrer and Laura Watson. Vine Books, 1993.

If Teacups Could Talk: Sharing a Cup of Kindness with Treasured Friends, Emilie Barnes. Harvest House, 1994.

Open Heart, Open Home, Karen Burton Mains. Cook Communications, 1991.

Things Happen When Women Care: Hospitality and Friendship in Today's Busy World, Emilie Barnes. Harvest House, 1990.

MARRIAGE

The Five Love Languages, Gary Chapman. Northfield Publishing, 1992.

The Gift of Sex, Cliff and Joyce Penner. Word Publishing, 1981.

Making Love Last Forever, Gary Smalley. Word Publishing, 1996.

Sex Begins in the Kitchen (Because Love Is an All-Day Affair), Dr. Kevin Leman. Baker Books, 1999.

Straight Talk to Men and Their Wives, Dr. James Dobson. Word Publishing, 1980.

Strike the Original Match, Chuck Swindoll. Tyndale House, 1989.

PARENTING

Bedtime Blessings: 100 Bedtime Stories & Activities for Blessing Your Child, John Trent. Focus on the Family, 2000.

Creative Correction, Lisa Whelchel. Tyndale House, 2000.

Daughters & Dads: Building a Lasting Relationship, Chap and Dee Clark. Navpress Publishing, 1998.

Focus on the Family Web site and resources, *www.family.org.*

Going Online @ Home, Ken Reaves. Broadman & Holman, 2000.

How to Pray for Your Children, Quinn Sherrer. Aglow, 1987.

Let's Make a Memory, Shirley Dobson and Gloria Gaither. Word Publishing, 1994.

Parenting Isn't for Cowards, Dr. James Dobson. Word Publishing, 1987.

Solid Answers, Dr. James Dobson. Tyndale House Publishers, Inc., 1997.

Successful Single Parenting, Gary Richmond. Harvest House, 1998.

PUBLIC POLICY/POLITICAL

CitizenLink, *www.citizenlink.org*

Citizen magazine, *www.family.org*

RECREATIONAL READING

The Mitford Series, by Jan Karon:

A Light in the Window, Penguin, 1995.

At Home in Mitford, Penguin, 1996.

These High Green Hills, Penguin, 1997.

Out to Canaan, Penguin, 1997.

A New Song, Viking Books, 1999.

A Common Life, Viking, 2001.

Left Behind: the Kids (series), Jerry B. Jenkins and Tim LaHaye. Tyndale House, 1998. The authors combine their interpretations of End Time events in Scripture with a fictional story.

Chronicles of Narnia (series), C. S. Lewis. Collier Books, 1986.

RELATIONSHIPS

The Friendship Factor, Alan LoyMcGinnes. Augsburg, 1979.

The Friendships of Women, Dee Brestin. Victor Books, 1988.

SPIRITUAL

Parents Guide to the Spiritual Mentoring of Teens, Eds. Joe White and Jim Weidmann. Tyndale House, 2001.

The Power of a Praying Wife, Stormie Omartian. Harvest House, 1997.

What Happens When We Pray for Our Families, Evelyn Christenson. Victor Books, 1992.

TIME MANAGEMENT

The Family Manager, Kathy Peel. Word Publishing, 1996.

The New Messies Manual: The Procrastinators Guide to Good Housekeeping, Sandra Felton. Revell, 2000.

Once-a-Month Cooking, Mimi Wilson and Mary Beth Lagerborg. Focus on the Family, 1984.

Survival for Busy Women, Emilie Barnes. Harvest House, 1986.

Working Women, Workable Lives, Karen Scalf Linamen and Linda Holland. Harold Shaw Publishers, 1993.

INDEX